What Others Say About Doug Giles

"Doug Giles brings the heat...as in the exact kind of refining heat the wussified church desperately needs. If you think he is too salty, then bless your heart but stay out of my foxhole because you aren't ready for the battle that has come to the door of the Church. But if you can handle the flames, then get ready to lock shields with Godly warriors called to push back evil at such a time as this. Doug will challenge, inspire, equip, offend, and embolden you...usually all at once and you'll love him for it. Welcome to the fight."

– Rick Green
Founder of Patriot Academy

"I think Doug Giles brings a sharp, humorous, bold and captivating style to ministry that strikes a chord with young people."

– Dr. R.C. Sproul

"There is NO way to describe Doug Giles adequately, so I won't even try. Suffice it to say there is NO ONE like him and I'm grateful for him!"

– Eric Metaxas

"Doug Giles speaks the truth ... he's a societal watchdog ... a funny bastard."

– Ted Nugent

"Doug Giles is a good man, and his bambinas are fearless. His girls Hannah and Regis Giles are indefatigable. I admire the Giles clan from afar."

– Dennis Miller

"Doug Giles must be some kind of a great guy if CNN wants to impugn him."

– Rush Limbaugh

"Doug Giles, the perfect dynamite needed to ignite a fire in the belly of every man, woman and child to live like warriors."

– Lieutenant Colonel Allen B. West

Dear Christian: Your Fear is Full of Crap

By Doug Giles

Table of Contents

Preface: Should Pastors Repent For Obeying Fauci?

Introduction: Some Pastors Called It "Wisdom."
I Called It "Fear."

Chapter One: I'll Eat A Tube Sock 1

Chapter Two: 17 Things Jesus Never Said 5

Chapter Three: God Didn't Make You A Coward 11

Chapter Four: The Righteous Are Bold As Lions 21

Chapter Five: The Big Government Beatitudes 29

Chapter Six: You Will Be Hated 33

Chapter Seven: We Must Obey God Rather
Than Men 49

Chapter Eight: Romans 13 & 1st Peter 2 55

Chapter Nine: Jesus & Social Distancing 69

Chapter Ten: 12 Days Of The Pandemic –
The Lord Fauci Version 77

Chapter Eleven: Anxiety Is A Sin. That Should
Worry You. 81

Chapter Twelve: Enlarged Through Distress 87

Chapter Thirteen: Shout At The Devil 97

Chapter Fourteen: The "F" Word 111

Chapter Fifteen: Jesus Promised Problems 129

Chapter Sixteen: The Warriors' Confession 139

Chapter Seventeen: Pastors Who Defied
The Ubiquitous COVIDictators 151

Chapter Eighteen: Here Are 49 More
Things To Shout At The Devil 169

Chapter Nineteen: Five Imprecatory Psalms
Against Wicked Leaders 175

Chapter Twenty: Satan Doesn't Want You Reading
This Chapter 189

The Biblical Badass Collection 207

About the Author 235

This book is dedicated to all the pastors who never played pandemic or stopped playing pandemic right after the "two weeks to flatten the curve" edict.

Preface: Should Pastors Repent For Obeying Fauci?

"If Jesus preached what ministers preach today He would've never been crucified."
– Leonard Ravenhill

Should pastors publicly repent, if they obeyed Fauci, in regard to how they conducted their ministry instead of adhering to the clear commands of the King of Kings and Lord of Lords?

That's a legit question, eh?

Fauci and his ilk advised churches to shut down and many churches shut down.

Fauci and his step-n-fetches all across "The Media" and in local, state, and federal governments said …

1. stop singing in person (Eph. 5:19),

2. stop hugging (Acts 20:37),

3. stop laying hands on the sick (Heb. 6:2),

4. stop in person preaching of the word (2Tim. 4:1-5)

5. stop communion (1Cor. 11:23-33),

6. stop greeting one another with a holy kiss (Rom. 16:16, 1Cor. 16:20, 2Cor. 13:12, 1Thess. 5:26, 1Pet. 5:14),

7. stop the weekly gathering together (Heb. 10:23-25)

8. skip rows/pews between other Christians and …

9. stop going out in public without a mask on.

… and a stack of pastors said … uh … okay.

You've got to be kidding me, pastor. You followed that clod instead of God?

Good luck explaining that to Jehovah when you rock up to the Bema Seat.

For pastors to obey that Big Government, China-beholden operator, also called Dr. Fauci, over the clear commands of the Captain of our Salvation is what the Greeks call *skubalon*; it is what is rendered in the Latin as *stercore tauri*; it is what good ol' Texans call bullcrap and it is what Jesus calls sin (Luke 12:4,5).

Yep, Jesus calls obeying men versus obeying God a big no-no. Indeed, that's not a wee little sin, reverend, but a T-Rex sized blunder that brings on God's hot -- and I mean hot -- displeasure (Mark 8:38).

In case your minister hasn't been paying attention to the evil cabal and their multifaceted machinations to cripple our country but has been instead jonesing on TikTok dance videos, here's a scant list of foul Fauci's infractions. Infractions that we all now know he knew. Of which, many rational people knew all along he knew, but were labeled "conspiracy theorists." We now have proof after his emails were exposed in June 2021 that we were right and Fauci was scamming us as in, big time. For instance …

1. Fauci knew the Chinese cooked up the Wuhan Wheezer in the Wuhan lab.

2. Fauci's "Gain of Function" money funded this

pernicious plague.

3. Fauci knew Hydroxychloroquine was safe and effective.

4. Fauci knew asymptomatic spreads do not occur.

5. Fauci knew the mask does squat against the spread of the virus.

6. Lord Fauci was chummy with Big Pharma in finding a "Cure/Vaccine" for the Chinavirus. A shot which, by the way, does nada to keep one from giving or getting the 'Rona cold.

7. And Fauci was all chummy with Big Tech regarding the censorship of sane people who dared to differ with his bogus blather.

Oh, by the way, and FYI: the source of the aforementioned 411 was Tony, himself. Yep, it was all disclosed in the emails. This was covered over at ClashDaily.com in articles like this one:

FINALLY: Even Liberal Sources Are Confirming Fauci's Role In Dubbing Lab Leaks 'A Conspiracy'

So, as asked of you early on: should a pastor who bowed the knee to Big Government bad cold edicts, based upon Fauci's specious "findings", publicly repent for not staying Christ's course during this scamdemic?

Pastor: How the heck do you resume your normal church services without saying to the church, "Hey, guys ... I messed up from 2020 - 2021+. I followed lies, hype, and spin. I bought into a mass delusional psychosis and I'm sorry to God and to you that I was a fear-laden stooge of the machine."

Not only should pastors repent for obeying what we all know now was hysterical nonsense regarding how Church should be conducted but also pastors should make this pledge to God and your congregation:

1. I will obey the word of God when it comes to how I conduct our worship services.

2. By the grace of God, I'll never be a gullible goober, ever again, as long as I live.

3. The Church I pastor will never stop singing in person (Eph. 5:19).

4. The Church I pastor will never stop hugging (Acts 20:37).

5. The Church I pastor will never stop laying hands on the sick (Heb. 6:2),

6. The Church I pastor will never stop in person preaching of the word (2Tim. 4:1-5).

7. The Church I pastor will never stop taking communion together (1Cor. 11:23-33),

8. The Church I pastor will never stop greeting one another with a holy kiss (Rom. 16:16, 1Cor. 16:20, 2Cor. 13:12, 1Thess. 5:26, 1Pet. 5:14).

9. The Church I pastor will never stop the weekly gathering together (Heb. 10:23-25).

10. The Church I pastor will never skip rows/pews between other Christians or make anyone wear a

mask because of some inane and insane, unbiblical, unscientific edict from a civil magistrate.

After taking The Pledge I recommend praying this prayer of contrition …

Lord Jesus. Please forgive me and I pray that You will give me holy testicular fortitude to be one of Your prophets versus one of Fauci's puppets. Again, I'm deeply sorry that I offended You by obeying the word of the government versus the Word of God. Please forgive me for the bad example I set for the body of Christ. In Jesus's name, amen.

Few pastors will confess their two-year bad cold obedience and cravenness to their congregations because they don't see being pusillanimous is a big whoop anymore and they have a totemic view of vice. Allow me to explain.

If a pastor was caught bumping uglies with some chick like Miley Virus we'd expect him to repent of his indiscretion and go get a big shot of penicillin, correct?

If a pastor lapsed into doing more drugs than Keith Richards on any given weekend, we'd expect remorse and contrition from the reverend before the congregation and then a prolonged stint at the Betty Ford Clinic, eh?

Furthermore, if a pastor had a nasty, vendetta spirit like that foul Twitter troll, Chrissy Teigen, who deals in death wishes and revels in *schadenfreude*, we'd expect that after the Holy Ghost convicts said pastor of being a spiteful crank that he'd publicly confess his dark heart to his congregation and then go Google up a good exorcist who could cast the devils out of him.

Lastly, if a pastor succumbed to the superfluity of naughtiness, as did Judas Iscariot, and absconded with the Church's funds, we'd expect upon conviction for him to confess before the sheep he'd been fleecing that he's been a bad boy and if allowed back into the ministry will refuse to take a salary or steal a penny from Christians from here on out.

You and I both know, in most churches, with most pastors, the above sins would warrant a public confession of folly because of their overt scandalous nature that's clearly condemned in scripture. That said, there are other sins clearly condemned in the *verbum Dei* that get nary a peep of condemnation by pastors and congregants who have a totemic view of vice. For instance, and apparently during the Bad Cold Charade, living in fear ain't a big deal anymore even though the injunction to "fear not" is the most profuse exhortation utilized in scripture. Also, kissing anti-Christian Big Government backside by obeying their counter-biblical edicts doesn't seem to be on the sassy pastors' hamartiological list of holy infractions nowadays, does it?

Nope, pastors and dull Christians don't see smooching Big Government butt as a big sin nowadays. Oh, no. They see taking marching orders from Fauci versus Jesus as "wisdom" and actually "obedience to God" in accordance with a severely twisted take on Rom. 13:1-7 and 1Pet. 2.13-17.

Their view of obeying, without question, civil magistrates is similar to the crack pastors smoked in pre-Nazi Germany right before the rise of the Third Reich. Google it if you don't believe me.

Also, in Acts chapter four, Peter, who said to obey leaders, told the leaders who were attempting to shut the church down to, effectively, go pound sand. Peter did not obey the governing officials when they officially went sideways against the commands of Christ. Duh.

Obviously, as you can tell, I think a *mea culpa* is in order from the pastors and priests who bailed on their post because an "expert" told them to during the bedamned and bedeviled bad cold days.

David, when busted by Nathan over his adultery and murder repented and said to all of Israel, "I'm the man." At least he was honest when convicted of his sin.

If you bowed to Big Government (sin) and blew off the clear commands in scripture to gather, travel, lay hands on the sick, etc. then you, like King David, sinned and should repent.

Pastor, if you call your fear and disobedience to the clear commands of Christ regarding when and how the church is to assemble no matter what bad cold is going around "wisdom and common sense" then you are …

A. Self-deceived.

B. In need of a double espresso to wake the heck up and …

C. In need of publicly repenting to your church.

Yep, pastor, if you, by example, tossed off your Christian duty and the Bill of Rights, in a scant four months in 2020, by obeying Fauci for any amount of time then you need to repent.

Some of you lost legit congregants because of your cowardice.

Don't blame your congregants for leaving when it was because you were being a tinkerpot instead of a defiant Son of Thunder, who understands that rebellion to tyrants is obedience to God.

The upshot, pastor, is God is a merciful and forgiving Father. He forgave Peter for his denial and greatly used him again, obviously. God's got a great track record of giving second chances, or rather, a gazillion chances to the repentant who acknowledge they screwed up by folding to fear and obeying an anti-Christian cabal during the ruse of the century.

Again, like any other sin that's confessed and forsaken, God is always there to forgive and restore the contrite who confess they blew it.

Introduction: Some Pastors Called It "Wisdom." I Called It "Fear."

"It has been well said that there are only three classes of people in the world today: those who are afraid, those who do not know enough to be afraid, and those who know their Bibles."
– Leonard Ravenhill

During the bad cold "crisis" of 2020 through 2021+ I saw many Christians cave into fear.

They went into lockdown-freak-out mode.

They "socially distanced" themselves from corporate worship and from pretty much everyone and everything else, except, of course, liquor, and grocery stores.

Pastors called it "wisdom".

They said we needed to obey Big Government for the "greater good". They called it, "loving their neighbor".

I called it "fear".

Uncut, irrational, unbiblical and not to mention, unconstitutional, fear.

Pure dread, pure terror, pure hysteria, and pure panic on a global scale.

We were assured that millions were gonna die if we disobeyed the government.

So, we shut down our epic economy.

We stopped attending our Sunday Services and decided to do it online via Facebook which happens to be no fan of Christianity or our Constitution.

We watched the news 24/7.

We watched the death counter rack up the numbers of supposed deaths caused by a bad cold.

We were told by Big Government goons, on April 7th, 2020, that we should stop shaking hands forever.

We were encouraged to rat out citizens who were disobedient to local magistrates. One weasel snitched on their neighbors who broke the new stay-at-home "laws" by daring to play catch with their little daughter at a deserted park.

We shunned thy neighbor and treated everyone like a diseased hooker because we were told it's "prudence" and based on "science".

I said, no, it's fear and you look stupid.

Some pastors who didn't bow their knee to the bad cold and close their churches were fined and/or arrested.

The "cure" was worse than the disease.

Some Christians blew off Jesus' call in Matthew 10:8 to cast out demons, heal the sick, and raise the dead and instead they opted for listening to demons, avoiding the sick, and counting the dead.

They obeyed men instead of God.

Some Christians stopped tithing and blew off their ecclesiastical commitments because of fear of the unknown. Unreal.

Thank God the fear-addled Christians weren't around during the bloody persecutions of the Church, or during the Revolutionary War when smallpox was ravaging our troops.

Or the less than yippy conditions during Martin Luther's Reformation.

Or when John Wycliffe enacted his epic work of translating the scriptures in jolly old England because he did that during the first leg of The Black Plague which wiped out 700-800,000 Brits.

If phobia-infused "believers" were around back then none of the great and glorious progress within the Church or the state would've been accomplished because they'd have been curled up in the fetal position, wetting their big-Christian diaper, afraid to act because they might get a runny nose.

Look folks, our founders and framers fought a war during a smallpox epidemic, and we gave away our freedoms in four short months because we were scared to catch a bad cold.

Speaking of our rowdy founders, Patrick Henry didn't say, "Give me liberty or give me death unless, of course, a serious case of the sniffles is going around and then I'll do exactly what the government tells me to do."

Also, please note that the First Amendment doesn't say, "Congress shall make no law respecting an establishment of religion, or prohibiting the free exercise thereof; unless there's a threat of getting sick for a couple of days."

Also, Jesus didn't say to obey Him only when it is convenient, and you're assured you won't suffer in this fallen world.

Look, I get the godless flipping out over getting sick. I don't get Christians wigging out. In Matt. 6:25-34, Jesus states that freaking out over the future is what the unwashed masses do, it's not what the Christian does.

Sure, the bad cold is/was real but so is the flu and it wipes out tens of thousands, year after year, and we don't stop life like we did with this relatively mild virus.

Life, in this fallen world, is going to toss us curveballs aplenty. Jesus promised storms, pain, persecution, and privation (Matt. 7:24-27). He also promised to protect and provide for them no matter what came (Matt. 6:25-33). To live in fear is to live in sin. Speaking of fear, one of the most repeated commands in scripture is, "fear not."

Chapter One: I'll Eat A Tube Sock

"If we displease God, does it matter who we please?
If we please Him does it matter whom we displease?"
– Leonard Ravenhill

Here's a challenge for the pastors and priests out there in the United States of Big Government Acrimony.

If you can show me one place in the scripture where Jesus, the prophets and/or the apostles said to …

1. Live in fear of a bad cold.

2. Live in fear of dying.

3. Live in fear of elected officials.

4. Obey civil magistrates who praise evil and punish good.

5. Stop singing, preaching, taking communion, and gathering together in person, if a bad cold starts coursing around the country.

6. If you do hold worship services, then mask up and skip rows/pews between families.

If you can show me, dear pastor and/or priest, one scripture that argues for any of the aforementioned ...

I'll eat a tube sock.

2020-2021+ was a black eye for a lot of ministers and churches.

A stack of pastors and priests obeyed draconian edicts that we now know didn't do diddly squat to stop the spread of the bad cold China released on the world.

- Businesses were wrecked.

- Churches were wrecked.

- Only a few ministers called BS on this mass delusional psychosis.

The ministers and Christians that went along with this Big Government ruse should be ashamed.

The ministers should repent to their congregation for being ...

1. Gullible instead of discerning.
2. Fearful instead of fearless.
3. For being a coward and too afraid to boldly confront the bad actors in the Bad-Cold Charade.

This book's intent is to help the Christian to never get fooled again into obeying an oppressive state and their specious demands the next time they come around and attempt to strap a rat cage on our collective heads.

Dear Christian: Your Fear is Full of Crap

Culture Warrior Battle Notes

Chapter Two: 17 Things Jesus Never Said

"The Church right now has more fashion than passion, is more pathetic than prophetic, is more superficial than supernatural."
– Leonard Ravenhill

"And I say unto thee, quarantine thyself, live in dread and flee from the sick for thou art an American Christian."
– Ringo 12:36

"Obey civil magistrates who don't give two flying craps about the Church."
– Specious Doo 6:66

"Hey, if there's a bad cold going around, stop meeting together, no more corporate gatherings, no more communion and singing and stuff."
– Snafu 2:32

"Rejoice, for God has given thee a spirit of fear, timidity, selfishness, and paranoia."
– Rosie 25:25

"When your conscience is telling you that the talking head on TV is full of more crap than a colicky baby's diaper, stifle that voice, buy what they're selling you, and ask for seconds."

— Dilbert 1:234.

"Don't worry about culture and politics and don't try to right this planet through evangelism and discipleship and the implementation of the biblical worldview because I'm about to blow up the globe and rescue my sad little church."

— Talking Heads 17:16

"We must obey men rather than God."

—Whiskey Tango Foxtrot 5:15

"Be feeble-minded and milk-livered when hard times come. Curl up in the fetal position and wet your big Christian diaper."

— el Diablo 37:11

"Your body is the temple of the Holy Spirit so inject it with strange concoctions that Herod wants you to take, and that are proven not to work."

— Slaves 78:17b

"Cover thy face with a dirty cloth like a good obedient zombie. Yay, wear it even when you're alone in your car."

— Billy Squire 867:5309

Dear Christian: Your Fear is Full of Crap

"When your nation is being taken over by anti-theistic goons, do not preach about it, or mention it during covered-dish dinners and act like it isn't really happening because you could get persecuted by big government droogies and you may very well upset some demonized old, rich chick that is in your church."

— Cerberus 2:42

"Get on the train. Everything will be okay."

— Pooh-Pooh el Grande 3:33

"Where the Spirit of the Lord is there is bondage to bad ideas and the fetid leaders who spawned them."

— Carrot Top 10:99

"Train up a child in the ways of civil magistrates and when they're old they will not depart from them."

— Gobbledygook 9:66

"Seek to be liked by crooked leaders just like Jesus and the prophets and the apostles did."

— WTF 45:54

"And I say unto thee do not, under any circumstance, teach on the biblical principles of liberty as found in the Constitution, Bill of Rights, and the Declaration of Independence because that could jeopardize thy non-profit status and/or tick off the left-leaning Marxists within your Church."

— Rotten Tomatoes 14:13.

"Hand thy children, whom thou lovest, over to radical communists (who hate that which is holy, just, and good) and let them educate your child in all things that pertaineth to this life."

— 2nd Skubalon 8:18

Dear Christian: Your Fear is Full of Crap

Culture Warrior Battle Notes

Chapter Three: God Didn't Make You A Coward

"A man who is intimate with God
is not intimidated by man."
– Leonard Ravenhill

To say that God is a generous giver is to understate a whopping big given.

Our two-cylinder gray matter will never be able to fully comprehend the magnitude of His generosity that He has lavished upon His former demon-driven, God-hating, thankless, fleshly, idol-worshiping enemies also known as you and me (Eph. 2:1-10).

God owes us nothing and yet decided to give us everything (Eph. 1:15-22).

According to the Bible, He's given His elect the following …

- His only begotten Son as our substitutionary sacrifice (John 3:16)

- The gift of faith (Eph. 2:8)

- The gift of repentance (Acts 5:31)

- The gift of grace (Eph. 2:8)

- The gift of the Word of God (Eph. 6:17)

- "Seeing eyes" (Matt. 13:16)

- "Hearing ears" (Matt. 13:16)

- The Holy Spirit (Acts 2:38)

- A glorious inheritance (Eph. 1:18)

- Eternal life (Rom. 6:23)

- A purpose on this planet (Rom. 8:28)

- A part in His demon-thrashing organism called, The Church (Matt. 16:18)

- Spiritual weapons and armor (Eph. 6:10-18)

- Supernatural power (2Pet. 1:3)

- Power over our flesh (Rom. 6:14)

- The authority to bind demonic forces (Matt. 18:18)

- His angelic army's assistance (Ps. 46:7)

- 24/7/365 access to His throne in prayer (Heb. 4:16)

- Fruit of the Holy Spirit (Gal. 5:22)

- Gifts of the Holy Spirit (1Cor. 12:4-11)

- Divine protection (Ps. 91)

- Covenant promises (2Pet. 1:4)

- Prosperity (3 John 2)

Dear Christian: Your Fear is Full of Crap

- Health (3 John 2)

- Healing (Isa. 53:5)

That's a pretty awesome little list that is far from an exhaustive account of what He's credited unto us simply because He's a good God and that's how He rolls (James 1:17).

There's one thing, however, if you have this character trait, then God did not give it to you.

Yep, if you're saddled with *this* crap, you didn't get it from Him.

You might have gotten this bent from talking too much to your aunt who's nuttier than a squirrel turd.

Or, perhaps, you now have this predilection because you listen to and believe what control freak politicians tell you.

Or, possibly, you are now saddled with this bunk because you take notes while watching "The News."

Whatever was the font from where you got this particular funk, it didn't come from our Heavenly Father.

So, what am I talking about, pray tell?

Well, you inquiring mind, I'm talking about the vomitus soup *du jour*, that a lot of Christians have eaten heapin' helpins of lately, namely: a spirit of fear.

Yes, Christians, who are called to fear not (Isa. 41:10) when in dire straits, tossed that notion aside around March 2020 and bought into what bureaucrats were selling us po' rubes, a thing Dr. Mark McDonald has deemed a "mass delusional psychosis", or what the Apostle Paul called, a spirit of fear (2Tim. 1:7).

Dear Church: What did Ray Davies teach us if he taught us anything at all, huh? He taught us that Paranoia Will Destroy Ya, and boy was he on point because fear of a bad cold and bad leaders did major, I said major, damage to the church, family, and state.

Hey, speaking of the church, show me one place in the scripture, Christian, where Jesus said to …

1. Fear getting a bad cold.
2. Obey a homunculus Italian "scientist" who tells you to skip Christmas this year and to wear a dirty rag over your face.
3. Shut your church down if a Mayor McCheese orders you to do it.

If you can show me one Bible verse that positively stumps for the aforementioned, I'll Riverdance in Borat's thong to an extended cut of The Doors smash hit, *Riders On The Storm.*

The Christian is never called to fear what this life tosses at them but to fear God and stand on His word instead (Lk.12:4,5). Sadly, a lot of the church flunked that test when the Wuhan Wheezer was unleashed on us by China and fell prey to satanic anxiety.

Fear is a sin, folks (Rev. 21:8). It's the antithesis of the Christian spirit of boldness (Prov. 28:1), hardiness (Heb. 10:32-36), righteous rebellion (Acts 5:29), and a gravity defying faith (Rom. 4:18).

Our great God would never give us some pathetic spirit of fear. That's horse crap. That's everything God isn't. Fear has jack squat to do with biblical faith and yet, there the church sat, for the last two years, obeying and doing ridiculous things because, they too, bought into a mass delusional psychosis and they called it "wisdom" and "loving their neighbor".

Unfortunately, two years later now, lo and behold, we find out that all those ridiculous mandated hoops the "experts" and politicians made churches jump through did not work to stop the spread of a bad cold.

Some pastors called kissing idiots' backsides during the days of the bad cold "being smart" and "gathering wisely". I call it being a wuss and acting stupid.

What you did, Pastor Disaster, wasn't wisdom. It wasn't love that made you cease corporate, in person, business as usual, essential/commanded worship. It was fear: 1. Fear they might catch a bad cold and 2. Fear if they ticked off their Mayor McCheese or their power trippin' governor they might get fined, go to jail, or lose their 501(c)3 that they worship more than God.

Whatever was the source of the pastor's dread that led them to obey and play pandemic with civil magistrates who hate the church, it sure as heck was not my King of Kings and my Lord of Lords.

For those still in a quandary whether God wants them to be a hamster saddled with a delusional psychosis or not, please peruse the various translations of one of my favorite scriptures, 2Tim.1:7.

For God did not give us a spirit of timidity (of cowardice, of craven and cringing and fawning fear), but [He has given us a spirit] of power and of love and of calm and well-balanced mind and discipline and self-control. (AMP)

You see, God did not give us a cowardly spirit but a powerful, loving, and disciplined spirit. (VOICE)

For God gave us a Spirit who produces not timidity, but power, love and self-discipline. (CJB)

God's Spirit doesn't make cowards out of us. The Spirit gives us power, love, and self-control. (CEV)

For God has not given us a spirit of cowardice, but of power, and of love, and of wise discretion. (DARBY)

The Spirit God gave us does not make us afraid. His Spirit is a source of power and love and self-control. (ERV)

For the Holy Spirit, God's gift, does not want you to be afraid of people, but to be wise and strong, and to love them and enjoy being with them. (TLB)

God gave us his Spirit. And the Spirit doesn't make us weak and fearful. Instead, the Spirit gives us power and love. He helps us control ourselves. (NIRV)

After all, the spirit given to us by God isn't a fearful spirit; it's a spirit of power, love and prudence. (NTE)

For why [Soothly] God gave not to us the spirit of dread, but of virtue, and of love, and of soberness. (WYC)

Did you catch that? Because I laid it down pretty thick. Pardon my redundancy but …

1. God did not give us a spirit of timidity (of cowardice, of craven and cringing and fawning fear).

2. God did not give us a cowardly spirit,

3. God's Spirit doesn't make cowards out of us.

4. The Spirit God gave us does not make us afraid.

5. For the Holy Spirit, God's gift, does not want you to be afraid of people (or a bad cold).

6. God gave us his Spirit. And the Spirit doesn't make us weak and fearful.

7. After all, the spirit given to us by God isn't a fear-

ful spirit.

8. For why [Soothly] God gave not to us the spirit of dread.

What God did give you Dinky was ...

1. **Power.** Yes Christian, if God truly invaded your life, then you can say *adios* to being timid, helpless, infirm, impotent, weak, powerless, and incompetent. That crap gets crucified when Christ moves into your castle and gets replaced with Holy Spirit dynamite (Acts 1:8).

2. **Love.** 1John 4:18 says, "perfect love casts out fear." The revelation of God's great love for us kills timidity before men and any fear of catching a bad cold. God's great love for us should make us holy and confident warriors who do not sweat what the unwashed masses sweat because our covenant keeping God deeply loves us and powerfully upholds and protects us.

3. **Sound Mind.** Yep, you read that correctly. God gives the believer a sound mind. But you wouldn't have known that because a lot of Christians acted the fearful fool and obeyed stupid bad cold rules and edicts and threw out their brain and common sense and fearfully played pandemic for two years. Instead of walking in the sound mind that God gave the Christian, many adopted the fear Fauci sold 'em. Shameful. Indeed, instead of not freaking out, many who claim to be believers bought the paranoia that "The News" peddled. *Ergo*, instead of having biblical peace in the midst of the storm, "Christians" became stressed, anxious, depressed, and suicidal because they believed public health officials versus the Word of God. This led to church closures, lockdowns, mask mandates, and vaccine mandates that we now know do not protect against getting or giving the bad cold to other peeps. All of the aforementioned came about because folks said "giddy up" to fear and "no thanks" to common sense and reason. Good job, tinkerpots.

Finally, say this next verse out loud and with some testicular fortitude.

> *"For God hath not given us the spirit of fear; but of power, and of love, and of a sound mind."*

Now say it again, louder!

> *"For God hath not given us the spirit of fear; but of power, and of love, and of a sound mind."*

Now say it again so loud that it startles yo' mama and she comes to see if you're ok.

> *"For God hath not given us the spirit of fear; but of power, and of love, and of a sound mind."*

Feels good, eh?

Lastly, put that scripture on your TV, laptop, and your smartphone and anytime some satanic fear-addled jackanape tries to offload their phobias on you, read that verse out loud again and then tell whoever is trying to get you to live in dread of men or a bad cold to go pound sand. In Christian love, of course.

Dear Christian: Your Fear is Full of Crap

Culture Warrior Battle Notes

Chapter Four: The Righteous Are Bold As Lions

*"Christianity today is so subnormal that if any
Christian began to act like a normal New Testament
Christian, he would be considered abnormal."*
– Leonard Ravenhill

According to someone who took the time to count them and put their findings online, supposedly, there are 915 proverbs in the *verbum Dei* and roughly 10% of them spotlight the difference between the wicked and righteous.

Solomon compares and contrasts the righteous and the wicked in such a clear way that someone with three teeth and an IQ of 50 could get what Solomon succinctly laid down regarding the signs of the wicked and the righteous.

For instance, Solomon says …

"The soul of the lazy one craves and gets nothing,
But the soul of the diligent is made prosperous."
Prov. 13:4 (NASB)

What's funny is, that nowadays, in hipster Christian churches, if there's some indolent evangelical dolt, who spouts off his grandiose dreams and yet produces nada because they're disinclined to get off their butt, we categorize them as someone who hasn't "unleashed their full potential yet" or "found their destiny." Solomon ain't so sweet in his assessment of said Sad Sack. No, Solomon says to the shiftless, you have nothing because you're a languorous clod (that's from The King Doug Translation of that scripture). In contrast with the Dudley Do-Nothings, Solomon says prosperity isn't a mystery laid upon the few but the by-product of having this thing that Generation Wussy is clearly devoid of, namely, diligence.

Another big difference between the righteous and the wicked, according to Solomon, is this ...

"A wise son accepts his father's discipline, But a scoffer does not listen to rebuke." Prov. 13:1 (NASB)

Did you catch that? A shrewd kid/person doesn't squeal when they get rebuked by their old man, or by God, or by their pastor, or by their boss. Yep, the wise and righteous person, doesn't take up an offense and pout and protest when someone chastises them for their chuckleheaded actions. They roll with the reprimand. The wicked, however, don't listen to rebuke. You can't correct them. They know it all.

Here's another example that'll get Solomon labeled a sexist by the hair triggered 5th wave feministas ...

"The wise woman builds her house, But the foolish tears it down with her own hands." Prov. 14:1 (NASB)

Dear Christian: Your Fear is Full of Crap

Oh, Good Lawd! Sol went there. He blamed a woman for the demise of a household. Is he nuts? Does he not know how politically incorrect that is? I guess not because he said, yes, women can, as well as men, wreck a family. If you don't believe Solomon just Google "Real Housewives of Orange County" and watch that drivel for about ten minutes.

Here's how The Passion Translation transliterates that verse ...

> *"Every wise woman encourages and builds up her family, but a foolish woman over time will tear it down by her own actions."*

So, in short, a wise woman inspires and motivates her husband and kids. A wicked woman is a contentious drip that eventually wrecks her husband and internally guts her poor kids. If that offends you, then I suggest you take it up with God because He's the one who inspired Solomon to put that in print (2Tim. 3:16).

Which brings me to the topic/verse this chapter is going to look at:

> *"The wicked flee when no one is pursuing, but the righteous are bold as a lion." Prov.28:1 (NASB)*

Solomon says that boldness is the trait of the righteous and the redeemed and fleeing is the trait of the wicked and the damned.

Here's a little interesting observation: You don't see Jesus fleeing when pursued by religious or political idiots or even Satan himself (Mark 1:13; Matt. 23). Matter of fact, and far from fleeing, Jesus regularly got up in their grill when they went full retard in His presence.

Same thing with John the Baptist. He wasn't characterized by sporting shriveled testicles and chewing his fingernails. John was bold (Matt. 11:7).

The same goes for the apostles and prophets. They were bold, salty dawgs (Acts 4:13; Acts 4:29).

Oh, and the biblical badass ladies were not characterized by being, "Oh, Beauregard!" wilting daisies, either. Mary, Hannah, Jael, Ruth, Rahab, Sarah, etc., were bold baby, bold!

Indeed, the biblical protagonists, lauded by Holy Writ, were bold before men and devils (Heb. 11:1-40). They were bold in their risk taking (Heb.11:8). They were bold in their love towards the unlovely (1Cor. 1:26-31). They were bold in the faith (Heb. 11:24-27). They were bold in their prayers (Acts 4:29).

They were bold with their sense of humor. Especially Elijah and Paul (1Kings 18:27; 1Cor. 4:8). Even in a culture that wanted to cancel them. Speaking of a sense of humor, comedian John Cleese of Monty Python fame, said, "Humor by its very nature is critical. And if you say there's a 'special' group of folks you can't offend then humor is gone and with humor goes a sense of proportion. And when that vanishes, as far as I'm concerned, you're living in 1984."

The biblical mainstays embodied what Dan. 11:32 says, … *"the people who know their God will be strong and take action."*

So, in case you're not getting it: the evil are fear-laden and craven; backward-looking hamsters and the Christlike are B-O-L-D, bold.

Do you need more proof? Check out this verse …

Dear Christian: Your Fear is Full of Crap

"... the cowardly, and unbelieving, and abominable, and murderers, and sexually immoral persons, and sorcerers, and idolaters, and all liars, their part will be in the lake that burns with fire and brimstone, which is the second death." Rev. 21:8 (NASB)

Did you catch whom Christ put first on the list of the damned? The cowardly. I doubt most sassy youth pastors would even see cowardice as that big of a deal anymore, but the Holy Spirit did and does.

People who truly collided with Christ were made instantly bold but now boldness seems to be the gift of the few when it was the common denominator of all the heroes and heroines of the scripture.

Nowadays, Christianity is all about being nice, not bold.

Would people characterize you as bold?

Solomon says the righteous don't just sport any old boldness but lion-like boldness. I've had the good fortune to have been around the big cats in my multiple travels to the Dark Continent. I've been on three African lion hunts, and I can tell you this with great certainty that they're not for the faint of heart. The lion I hunted came at full charge to kill us. Their roar/grunts, as they come for you, will leave what Kramer on Seinfeld called, "memory burn."

Please Note: There're ¾ of a million words used in the scripture and the Holy Spirit inspired Solomon to compare the Christian with a lion.

Most Christians just focus on us being little sheep where Solomon says, *au contraire*, the righteous are bold as lions. If we are sheep, we're sheep to God alone. To men and devils, we're dangerous apex holy predators akin to lions.

So, why would Solomon say the Christian is lion-like in their boldness? Well, maybe it's because Jesus is called the Lion of the Tribe of Judah. Rev. 5:5. Hello.

Jesus is not called the Koala Bear of Judah. He's not called the Hello Kitty of Judah. He's not called the Cuddly Monkey of Judah, or the Pronghorn Antelope, or Turtle Dove, or Panda Bear of Judah. He's called the Lion of The Tribe of Judah.

Since we're called to be like Him and it's the Holy Ghost's job to morph us into His image (Rom. 8:29) then, ipso facto, we, too, will exhibit lionlike boldness when we get stuck between a rock and a hard place versus fleeing like a frickin' little quail.

Can I get an amen?

Dear Christian: Your Fear is Full of Crap

Culture Warrior Battle Notes

Chapter Five: The Big Government Beatitudes

"Is the world crucified to you or does it fascinate you?"
– Leonard Ravenhill

Blessed are the gullible in spirit, for theirs is the great deception.

Blessed are those who're lazy, for they will be the receptor of government cheese.

Blessed are the blame shifters, for they will inherit a van down by the river.

Blessed are those who hunger and thirst for self-pity, for they will be Bernie bros.

Blessed are the woke, for they shall go broke.

Blessed are the social media junkies for they will grow man tits and live with mommy forever.

Doug Giles

Blessed are the Marxist devotees, for they shall be called useful idiots.

Blessed are those who are persecuted because of bad ideas, for theirs is the wrong side of history.

Dear Christian: Your Fear is Full of Crap

Culture Warrior Battle Notes

Chapter Six: You Will Be Hated

*"One thing and one thing alone keeps us from
complete decay in this hour – the church, the true
Church."*
– Leonard Ravenhill

In Acts chapter three, God used Peter to heal a lame beggar who asked Pete for cash but got healed by the Holy Spirit instead (Acts 3:1-9). The now-healed amigo had been crippled since birth so, as you can imagine, he's freaking out with joy, the onlooking crowd is freaking out with fear and Peter's like … "that's how we roll, baby."

Peter then blasts the spectating men of Israel for their rejection of Jesus and then the whole place gets lit and this miraculous healing turns into a riot and jail time for Peter and John.

Not too shabby, eh?

To me, that little soiree beats the heck out of your typical business as usual sucky church service.

Can I get a witness?

So, following on the heels of Acts chapter three is Acts

chapter four (KJV) and this chapter is a doozy. Check it out…

1 And as they spake unto the people, the priests, and the captain of the temple, and the Sadducees, came upon them,

2 Being grieved that they taught the people, and preached through Jesus the resurrection from the dead.

3 And they laid hands on them, and put them in hold unto the next day: for it was now eventide.

4 Howbeit many of them which heard the word believed; and the number of the men was about five thousand.

5 And it came to pass on the morrow, that their rulers, and elders, and scribes,

6 And Annas the high priest, and Caiaphas, and John, and Alexander, and as many as were of the kindred of the high priest, were gathered together at Jerusalem.

7 And when they had set them in the midst, they asked, By what power, or by what name, have ye done this?

8 Then Peter, filled with the Holy Ghost, said unto them, Ye rulers of the people, and elders of Israel,

9 If we this day be examined of the good deed done to the impotent man, by what means he is made whole;

10 Be it known unto you all, and to all the people of Israel, that by the name of Jesus Christ of Nazareth, whom ye crucified, whom God raised from the dead, even by him doth this man stand here before you whole.

11 This is the stone which was set at nought of you builders, which is become the head of the corner.

12 Neither is there salvation in any other: for there is none other name under heaven given among men, whereby we must be saved.

13 Now when they saw the boldness of Peter and John, and perceived that they were unlearned and ignorant men, they marvelled; and they took knowledge of them, that they had been with Jesus.

14 And beholding the man which was healed standing with them, they could say nothing against it.

15 But when they had commanded them to go aside out of the council, they conferred among themselves,

16 Saying, What shall we do to these men? for that indeed a notable miracle hath been done by them is manifest to all them that dwell in Jerusalem; and we cannot deny it.

17 But that it spread no further among the people, let us straitly threaten them, that they speak henceforth to no man in this name.

18 And they called them, and commanded them not to speak at all nor teach in the name of Jesus.

19 But Peter and John answered and said unto them, Whether it be right in the sight of God to hearken unto you more than unto God, judge ye.

20 For we cannot but speak the things which we have seen and heard.

21 So when they had further threatened them, they let them go, finding nothing how they might punish them, because of the people: for all men glorified God for that which was done.

22 For the man was above forty years old, on whom this miracle of healing was shewed.

23 And being let go, they went to their own company, and reported all that the chief priests and elders had said unto them.

24 And when they heard that, they lifted up their voice to God with one accord, and said, Lord, thou art God, which hast made heaven, and earth, and the sea, and all that in them is:

25 Who by the mouth of thy servant David hast said, Why did the heathen rage, and the people imagine vain things?

26 The kings of the earth stood up, and the rulers were gathered together against the Lord, and against his Christ.

27 For of a truth against thy holy child Jesus, whom thou hast anointed, both Herod, and Pontius Pilate, with the Gentiles, and the people of Israel, were gathered together,

28 For to do whatsoever thy hand and thy counsel determined before to be done.

29 And now, Lord, behold their threatenings: and grant unto thy servants, that with all boldness they may speak thy word,

30 By stretching forth thine hand to heal; and that signs and wonders may be done by the name of thy holy child Jesus.

31 And when they had prayed, the place was shaken where they were assembled together; and they were all filled with the Holy Ghost, and they spake the word of God with boldness. (KJV)

Pretty epic, eh? Peter and John morphed into two biblical badasses, didn't they?

Herewith are four little ditties I've wrung out of those thirty-one verses from Acts 4.

Number One: If you're truly following Jesus and you are preaching the gospel, as is, without any 21st century fluff, I have some advice for you: Log on to Amazon.com and buy an athletic protective cup because it is going to get rough. Yep, brace yourself for persecution. Especially in these bedeviled days.

Folks, Peter and John were arrested.

If they were around today, they would still be arrested.

Dear Christian: Your Fear is Full of Crap

Or at least they'd be canceled by the oh so lame Thought Police.

They definitely would be banned from Herr Zuckerberg's Facebook and deplatformed by the twits at Twitter.

Back in 1974, Bad Company posed a question, in their famous song, namely ... Are you ready for love?

Two thousand years ago, Jesus would often warn and ask the disciples, not are you ready for love, but are you ready for the hatred that's going to come to those who truly follow Me?

As Geddy Lee aptly sang, if you "catch the spirit" you'll "catch the spit."

Alright, I'll quit quoting epic 1970's rock bands. Anyway ...

Peter and the boys were hated by the political and religious power brokers, for a good deed and speaking the truth to power, just as Jesus said they would be. Check it out.

> *18 "If the world hates you, you know that it has hated Me before it hated you. 19 If you were of the world, the world would love you as its own; but because you are not of the world, but I chose you out of the world, because of this the world hates you. 20 Remember the word that I said to you, 'A slave is not greater than his master.' If they persecuted Me, they will persecute you as well; if they followed My word, they will follow yours also.." John 15:18-20 (NASB)*

God used Peter to heal a famous crippled beggar and then Peter preached to the crowd and that instigated the wrath of man.

So, the apostles were hated.

Jesus was hated.

Are you hated?

If not, you ain't doing your Christianity Jesus-style because they loathed that thirty-year-old Rebel from Galilee.

Leonard Ravenhill famously said, "If Jesus preached what ministers preach today, He would've never been crucified."

Goofy PC Pastors love to be loved.

They love to get "thumbs ups" on social media.

They loved to be ogled.

Which leads them to do three things:

1. Embrace political correctness.

2. Buy massive amounts of butt-kisser lip balm.

3. Deny Christ and be ashamed of His tough statements.

Jesus had a particular warning to the feckless who have a fondness for being fawned over.

> "Woe to you when all men speak well of you, for their fathers used to treat the false prophets in the same way." Luke 6:26 (NASB)

Check out how other translations bark that verse.

> How terrible for you when all speak well of you. Their ancestors did the same things to the false prophets. (CEB)

Dear Christian: Your Fear is Full of Crap

You are in for trouble when everyone says good things about you. That is what your own people said about those prophets who told lies. (CEV)

How bad it is when everyone says nothing but good about you. Just look at the false prophets. Their ancestors always said good things about them. (ERV)

And what sadness is ahead for those praised by the crowds—for false prophets have always been praised. (TLB)

There's trouble ahead when you live only for the approval of others, saying what flatters them, doing what indulges them. Popularity contests are not truth contests—look how many scoundrel preachers were approved by your ancestors! Your task is to be true, not popular. (MSG)

What sorrow awaits you who are praised by the crowds, for their ancestors also praised false prophets. (NLT)

Jesus said the dude, or dudette, who everyone likes is a false prophet.

Guess where false prophets go upon expiration?

Hint: it's not heaven.

I wonder how many 21st century hipster Christian pastors have Luke 6:26 tattooed on their skinny arms or around their pencil neck?

I literally heard a group of church leaders say of their pastor that one of the reasons they chose him to be their leader is because (unlike Jesus, the prophets and the apostles) everyone likes him.

By the way, make sure you're hated for the right reasons. Some of you are hated, but for all the wrong reasons (1Pet. 2:20).

I knew this obnoxious Jehovah Witness dude in high school who went around haranguing people about his stupid Watchtower Magazine and becoming part of "Jehovah's 144,000 Saints."

No one liked him and it wasn't because he was such a godly example of spiritual yumminess but because he was a non-stop, unbathed, zombie-eyed pain in the ass. He wasn't being persecuted because he was saintly. He was being rightly not loved because he was a repugnant cultist.

Speaking of Jehovah Witnesses.

Do you know what you get when you cross a Jehovah Witness with an agnostic?

Someone who knocks on your door for no apparent reason.

Back to our text …

Please note that Dr. Luke reported that, *"The enemy conspired how to get rid of them (Peter and John)."*

If you're worth your salt, the enemy will conspire against you.

If you're a crowd-pleasing little dipstick Christian, you can relax because the Devil and his ilk won't machinate against you because you're one of their ubiquitous useful idiots.

Another point I'd like to brand on the reader's brain is: Peter and John's preaching of the Resurrection meant that *Jesus* was King of Kings and Lord of Lords and *not* Caesar. And therein lies the rub.

In Pete's day, saying "Jesus is Lord" was an ecclesiastical and political offense. The priests, the captain of the temple guard and the Sadducees were "greatly disturbed" by their preaching of Christ's Lordship in all areas of life. Why did they get their panties in a bunch? Well, once again, the first century disciples hailed Christ as King and not Caesar. They obeyed Jesus' word over Caesar's edicts. Which is weird because twenty first century Christians do the opposite. If some mere human magistrate tells a groovy Christian something that goes against Gospel grain the go-along-to-get-along Christian obeys civil magistrates instead of Lord Jesus and we saw a crap ton of that go down in churches from 2020-2021+.

Indeed, 1st century Christianity was an offense to Roman rule. I'll expound more on that topic in the next chapter. Stay tuned …

Number Two. Please note when governments and corrupt religion are coming after you and the message, it is harvest time. Difficult times equal ripe harvest conditions. If you don't believe me, re-read Acts 4 and give Matt. 9:36-38 a gander.

Check this out.

> *"And they laid hands on them and put them in prison until the next day, for it was already evening. But many of those who had heard the message believed; and the number of the men came to be about five thousand." Acts 4:3-4 (NASB)*

Persecution equaled a lot of folks getting converted.

Peter and John, being very politically incorrect, preaching Christ's Lordship against the punks of the Roman state, equated a massive stack of peeps getting converted. By the way, they got saved knowing what they were saying "yes" to was a big no-no to the Roman ruled government and the religious hoity-toity.

Maybe if we preached what Peter and John did back in the day, we too would see a massive revival of folks converted to the Lord Jesus and no longer beholden to our current bevy of big government "Caesars".

Number Three. God used "Uneducated and untrained men."

> *"Now as they observed the confidence of Peter and John and understood that they were uneducated and untrained men, they were amazed, and began to recognize them as having been with Jesus." Acts 4:13 (NASB)*

The arrogant and specious religious "experts" said Peter and John were "uneducated and untrained men".

Uneducated and untrained?

Uh, earth to religious experts.

Peter and John *were* educated, and they *were* trained. They were educated and trained by The Master, you morons.

I love the fact that their bold and defiant confidence was noted as the resultant effect of having "been with Jesus".

Nowadays, having "been with Jesus" has been bastardized into the exact opposite of how Peter and John grooved. Yes, today, when someone has "been with Jesus" they come out passive, compliant to bad ideas, and tenebrous.

Another reason I love the fact that these wizards referred to Peter and John as "unlearned and untrained". It gives me great hope because I, too, was a Beavis back in the day and yet, God has used my haggard life for His glory.

I find it funny that these two rubes were used to shake nations and write divinely inspired scripture that has wreaked havoc on Satan's crumbling kingdom for many, many moons.

John was so dumb that he wrote the book of John which has been hailed as "the Plato of the New Testament". To further prove what a knucklehead John was he wrote 1st,

2nd, and 3rd John. And to really demonstrate what a goofball John was he wrote The Book of Revelation which baffles all the wise men.

Another glorious thing about Peter and John's usage was just a few months prior to Acts 4 both of them had denied Christ and were in fear for their lives and yet, Jesus restored them and used them greatly. Can you say, boom?!?

God used them mightily after a mass failure.

God nearly always picks from the back of the line.

God uses the base and the corrupt to heal, preach and flip the world upside down.

That's me and you, baby.

> *26 For consider your calling, brothers and sisters, that there were not many wise according to the flesh, not many mighty, not many noble; 27 but God has chosen the foolish things of the world to shame the wise, and God has chosen the weak things of the world to shame the things which are strong, 28 and the insignificant things of the world and the despised God has chosen, the things that are not, so that He may nullify the things that are, 29 so that no human may boast before God. 30 But it is due to Him that you are in Christ Jesus, who became to us wisdom from God, and righteousness and sanctification, and redemption, 31 so that, just as it is written: "Let the one who boasts, boast in the Lord 1Cor. 1:26-31 (NASB)*

Number Four. And lastly, please note that "being filled with the Holy Spirit" made Peter and John bold. Yep, when the Holy Ghost moves into your meat suit you will stand up to big government goons who want to shut you down.

In case you have short term memory problems, here it is again.

Acts 4:5-31 (KJV)

5 And it came to pass on the morrow, that their rulers, and elders, and scribes,

6 And Annas the high priest, and Caiaphas, and John, and Alexander, and as many as were of the kindred of the high priest, were gathered together at Jerusalem.

7 And when they had set them in the midst, they asked, By what power, or by what name, have ye done this?

8 Then Peter, filled with the Holy Ghost, said unto them, Ye rulers of the people, and elders of Israel,

9 If we this day be examined of the good deed done to the impotent man, by what means he is made whole;

10 Be it known unto you all, and to all the people of Israel, that by the name of Jesus Christ of Nazareth, whom ye crucified, whom God raised from the dead, even by him doth this man stand here before you whole.

11 This is the stone which was set at nought of you builders, which is become the head of the corner.

12 Neither is there salvation in any other: for there is none other name under heaven given among men, whereby we must be saved.

13 Now when they saw the boldness of Peter and John, and perceived that they were unlearned and ignorant men, they marvelled; and they took knowledge of them, that they had been with Jesus.

14 And beholding the man which was healed standing with them, they could say nothing against it.

15 But when they had commanded them to go aside out of the council, they conferred among themselves,

16 Saying, What shall we do to these men? for that indeed a notable miracle hath been done by them is manifest to all them that dwell in Jerusalem; and we cannot deny it.

17 But that it spread no further among the people, let us

straitly threaten them, that they speak henceforth to no man in this name.

18 And they called them, and commanded them not to speak at all nor teach in the name of Jesus.

19 But Peter and John answered and said unto them, Whether it be right in the sight of God to hearken unto you more than unto God, judge ye.

20 For we cannot but speak the things which we have seen and heard.

21 So when they had further threatened them, they let them go, finding nothing how they might punish them, because of the people: for all men glorified God for that which was done.

22 For the man was above forty years old, on whom this miracle of healing was shewed.

23 And being let go, they went to their own company, and reported all that the chief priests and elders had said unto them.

24 And when they heard that, they lifted up their voice to God with one accord, and said, Lord, thou art God, which hast made heaven, and earth, and the sea, and all that in them is:

25 Who by the mouth of thy servant David hast said, Why did the heathen rage, and the people imagine vain things?

26 The kings of the earth stood up, and the rulers were gathered together against the Lord, and against his Christ.

27 For of a truth against thy holy child Jesus, whom thou hast anointed, both Herod, and Pontius Pilate, with the Gentiles, and the people of Israel, were gathered together,

28 For to do whatsoever thy hand and thy counsel determined before to be done.

29 And now, Lord, behold their threatenings: and grant unto thy servants, that with all boldness they may speak thy word,

30 By stretching forth thine hand to heal; and that signs and wonders may be done by the name of thy holy child Jesus.

31 And when they had prayed, the place was shaken where they were assembled together; and they were all filled with the Holy Ghost, and they spake the word of God with boldness.

Being filled with the Holy Spirit played out in Peter and John's life with that dynamic duo showcasing great acts of boldness, confidence, and zero fear of civil magistrates (Acts 4:8; 13; 16-31).

Here's a question for you: Do you think if Peter and John were around today and some power trippin' governor told them to shut their church down because people might catch a cold that P&J would comply?

Uh, I … think … not.

Jesus wouldn't have obeyed that request either. Nor Paul or any of the other epic apostles or prophets.

They showed boldness in the face of persecution.

They rebuked and disobeyed their leaders who wanted them to be nice and mild, silent and compliant, little Christians.

Culture Warrior Battle Notes

Chapter Seven: We Must Obey God Rather Than Men

"At this grim hour, the world sleeps in the darkness, and the Church sleeps in the light."
– Leonard Ravenhill

24 Now when the captain of the temple guard and the chief priests heard these words, they were greatly perplexed about them as to what would come of this. 25 But someone came and reported to them, "The men whom you put in prison are standing in the temple area and teaching the people!" 26 Then the captain went along with the officers and proceeded to bring them back without violence (for they were afraid of the people, that they might be stoned).

27 When they had brought them, they had them stand before the Council. The high priest interrogated them, 28 saying, "We gave you strict orders not to continue teaching in this name, and yet, you have filled Jerusalem with your teaching and intend to bring this Man's blood upon us." 29 But Peter and the apostles answered, "We must obey God rather than men. (Acts 5:24-29)

Did you catch that last sentence, fair Christian?

The authorities told Peter and the apostles to stop preaching.

Peter told them to take a long walk off a short pier.

Check out these other treatments of that beautiful passage.

Peter and the apostles replied: We don't obey people. We obey God. (CEV)

But Peter answering, and the apostles, said, God must be obeyed rather than men. (DARBY)

Peter and the other apostles answered, "We must obey God, not human authority! (EXB)

Then Peter and the apostles answered him, "It is our duty to obey the orders of God rather than the orders of men. (PHILLIPS)

Peter and the Apostles: If we have to choose between obedience to God and obedience to any human authority, then we must obey God. (VOICE)

Verse 29 would make a badass refrigerator magnet, eh?

Y'know … a little inspiration and information regarding what to do when draconian goons come back for round two of the lockdowns?

Here's something that isn't mentioned that much in our nicer-than-Christ-Churches but is highlighted greatly throughout the Book of Acts: The Christians of the first century were rebels with a cause. They weren't the hair-spray-addicted, religious sponges of pop culture and oppressive governments looking to be ogled by an Oprah-addled crowd. Oh, no, *señorita*. The primitive church was out to change the world.

After Jerusalem fell in AD 70, the church, birthed by the

Dear Christian: Your Fear is Full of Crap

Holy Spirit during Rome's heyday, exploded with growth in Asia Minor — which happened to be Ground Zero for Caesar worship.

The punch-drunk citizens of Roman rule thought the various Caesars, their laws, and their government were God. They built temples to these men and minted coins with their mugs stamped on them. The poor dupes of Rome believed their leaders' poop didn't stink and they could do no wrong. They even gave their human leaders godlike reverence, proclaiming Caesar as Savior and Healer, King of Kings and Lord of Lords.

Yep, to the serfs of Caesarland, their heads of state were just dreamy, and as they were divine everyone was expected to toe their line. Because of this blind faith in Caesar, the Roman government found it a piece of cake to tax the plebes to death, snatch their kids or their houses, and create crises that ginned up even more robust control of Rome's citizens. I'm talkin' Caesar had them on a short leash because of their faith in the state. Sound familiar?

The early church, however, made it clear amidst this crapola that their allegiance was to Christ and not the edicts of Caesar — especially when Caesar's dictates conflicted with the Word of God. Yep, it was the church's disdain for Caesar's unrighteous decrees (the decrees that required their obedience at the expense of their convictions) that got them killed.

Get it right, folks: It wasn't the church's belief that Jesus is God, or their love of covered-dish dinners, or their Christian rock music that got them the ax; it was their holy defiance to the demonic edicts that Caesar attempted to slap them with. Rome didn't give a rat's backside who or what they believed in just as long as that belief didn't rock the boat of the Roman state. And that's exactly what first century Christianity did: It adhered to God's laws versus

Rome's. The Church believed that Christ was Lord and therefore, respectfully of course, Caesar could kiss their fish sticker. Indeed, following the teachings of Jesus, the initial Ichthus crowd was cantankerous when it came to an oppressive state.

I'm sure the church tried to be nice about their obstinacy toward Rome's odious laws, but when push came to legislative shove and it became clear that Caesar was requiring them to walk his way versus God's, the first century church defied the state instead of denying their God.

Oh, but I can hear it now. Some little timid pastor is thinking … but … but … but what about Romans 13 and 1st Peter 2 that tell us to obey our leaders? Good question, Dinky. I'll examine those two passages in my next chapter.

So, hold on to your lug nuts. It's time for an overhaul.

Dear Christian: Your Fear is Full of Crap

Culture Warrior Battle Notes

Chapter Eight: Romans 13 & 1st Peter 2

"But you know if God should stamp eternity or even judgment on our eyeballs, or if you'd like on the fleshy table of our hearts I am quite convinced we'd be a very, very different tribe of people, God's people, in the world today. We live too much in time, we're too earth bound. We see as other men see, we think as other men think. We invest our time as the world invests it. We're supposed to be a different breed of people. I believe that the church of Jesus Christ needs a new revelation of the majesty of God. We're all going to stand one day, can you imagine it- at the judgment seat of Christ to give an account for the deeds done in the body. This is what- this is the King of kings, and He's the Judge of judges, and it's the Tribunal of tribunals, and there's no court of appeal after it. The verdict is final."
– Leonard Ravenhill

13 Every person is to be subject to the governing authorities. For there is no authority except from God, and those which exist are established by God.

2 Therefore whoever resists authority has opposed the ordinance of God; and they who have opposed will receive condemnation upon themselves. 3 For rulers are not a cause of fear for good behavior, but for evil. Do you want to have no fear of authority? Do what is good and you will have praise from the same; 4 for it is a servant of God to you for good. But if you do what is evil, be afraid; for it does not bear the sword for nothing; for it is a servant of God, an avenger who brings wrath on the one who practices evil. Rom. 13:1-4 (NASB)

13 Submit yourselves for the Lord's sake to every human institution, whether to a king as the one in authority, 14 or to governors as sent by him for the punishment of evildoers and the praise of those who do right. 1Pet. 2:13-14 (NASB)

I hope you pay close attention to this chapter. It could save your life, revive the church, and right our nation.

My dad used to tell me all the time, "Boy ... you'd better pay attention. If you don't pay attention, you're going to pay somebody."

We had an older friend in Miami who never paid attention to anything. Completely oblivious to what was said or done around him. His name was Morris. When he was 82 years old, he went to his doctor for a general checkup. A few days later Morris' doctor saw him walking down the street with a hot young blonde babe on his arm. The following morning the doctor bumps into Morris again at the coffee shop and he said, "Morris! Looks like you are doing good, there brother! Morris said, "I sure am, doc. I'm doing exactly what you told me to do, get a hot mama and be cheerful!" The doctor replied, "Morris ... I said you have a heart murmur and be careful."

Dear Christian: Your Fear is Full of Crap

During The Bad Cold Charade of 2020-2021+ a lot of ministers used the aforementioned verses as proof texts to why they should believe and obey the lies, hype and spin coming from the governmental wizards about the corona cold.

They said, "Paul and Peter said we'd better obey our Mayor McCheese or we're going to tick God off and you know how He gets when He's angry."

So there they went. Shutting their churches down.

Wearing ineffective dirty masks and social distancing.

If churches did gather together, they stopped communion, corporate singing, and hugging and stuff and just weirdly walked around each other, grinning like everything's normal, while covered in Purell, opening doors with their elbows, and shuffling around like Sleestaks from the *Land of the Lost*.

Some churches climbed aboard the vaxx train which has now been proven an empty caboose, completely ineffective, to keep one from either getting or transmitting the Chinese sniffles. Matter of fact, a study out of the UK says 90% of the bad cold deaths were amongst the vaccinated. Hello. "REPORT: 90% Of COVID Deaths Are Among The VACCINATED — Here's The 411" https://clashdaily.com/2022/03/report-90-of-covid-deaths-are-among-the-vaccinated-heres-the-411/

And the pastors and Christians did all of the above because of a big case of demon-inspired fear and a misinterpretation of Romans 13 and 1Peter 2.

And folks still say, "theology doesn't matter."

The heck it doesn't.

Sound doctrine can keep you clipping with a sound mind when everybody and their chihuahua are acting like irrational hamsters.

Some pastors and churches looked like freaked out fools for months and months because they couldn't or wouldn't "rightly divide the word of truth" (2Tim.2:15) when it came to the passages in Romans 13 and 1st Peter.

In this chapter, we'll peel apart those texts to see if indeed they command the Christian to obey every edict the government doles out.

Some churches say, "Yea!"

The scriptures say, "Nay!"

Here's an FYI: The greatest threat to the church is bad government and churches who're in lockstep with those power tripping jackanapes.

Oh, by the way, when's the last time you heard, from the main pulpit, during a regular service, a sermon about the Christian's duty to resist bad government?

What's that I hear?

Do I hear crickets?

Yep, I thought so.

Hmmm. I wonder why?

Unlike Morris, listen carefully to what Paul says in Romans 13:1-4 (NASB).

13 Every person is to be subject to the governing authorities. For there is no authority except from God, and those which exist are established by God. 2 Therefore whoever resists authority has opposed the ordinance of God; and they who have opposed will receive condemnation upon themselves. 3 For rulers are not a cause of fear for good behavior, but for evil. Do you want to have no fear of authority? Do what is good and you will have praise from the same; 4 for it is a servant of God to you for good.

Dear Christian: Your Fear is Full of Crap

But if you do what is evil, be afraid; for it does not bear the sword for nothing; for it is a servant of God, an avenger who brings wrath on the one who practices evil.

Let's break it down, shall we?

1. The role of government is to restrain evil, not legislate it. Hello. Did you catch that? Only, according to the scripture, when government restrains what is evil (as defined by the scripture) is it doing what God ordained it to do. Duh.

2. Government is a necessary tool of God to restrain human clods from doing wicked garbage. That's it.

3. Paul also informs us in Rom. 13:3-4 that if you're doing what's right, you're protected but if you're doing what is evil … eh, not so much.

4. Also, did you catch the part in verse three where Paul says a God ordained government "praises" folks who do good? Again, good as defined by the scripture not by woke Marxists. It doesn't say it harasses folks living righteously. It doesn't say it fines them for living bold and free during the Wuhan wheezer. Only rogue, civil magistrates, badger good people, not God ordained governing authorities. God ordained authorities only put the sword to evil people. Y'know … like people who lie, oppress, steal, strangle your freedom, crush your business, and shut down your church.

So, that's God's idea of good government.

Ergo, my beloved, when the authorities cease to praise good and crush evil, you're not duty bound to obey that "authority" because they have abnegated God's delegated design. Does that make sense to you? It does to *moi*.

Oh, by the way, in case you can't read or haven't read the book of Acts or Paul's epistles because you either illiterate and/or dilatory, Paul, the author of Romans 13, bounced in and out of jail more than Lindsey Lohan did from 2007 through 2013. Indeed, Paul wore county orange more than any other preacher in the entire New Testament. They finally had to chop his noggin off because they couldn't shut him up. Every time they'd try to stifle him, beat him, toss him in the clink thinking that'll dial him down, Paul, like a faithful old Timex, took a licking and kept on ticking.

Now let's look at 1st Pedro 2:13-14.

Submit yourselves for the Lord's sake to every human institution, whether to a king as the one in authority, or to governors as sent by him for the punishment of evildoers and the praise of those who do right.

Here's a couple of observations from those twain texts.

1. When we submit to authority, it's for "the Lord's sake." Translation? Well, when the governing bodies are doing what God called them to do your best bet is to fall in line and submit to 'em. Conversely, when it ain't, then you don't. You dig?

2. What is the role of earthly authority? It's two-fold: a). Punish evildoers and b). cheerlead for those who live righteously. Again, and pardon my re-

dundancy, evil and good as defined by the scripture and not a lawless land.

Lastly, Peter, like Paul, who exhorted us to obey good government, also bounced in and out of prison for disobeying bad government.

Their motto was, "We must obey God rather than men."

Tattoo that on your bicep.

For the fair and squishy Pastor who still thinks they should always obey civil magistrates without question, after reading that world-class exegesis I just performed on Romans 13 and 1 Peter 2, I give you a few more examples of holy rebellion.

> *Then the king of Egypt spoke to the Hebrew midwives, one of whom was named Shiphrah, and the other was named Puah; and he said, "When you are helping the Hebrew women to give birth and see them upon the birthstool, if it is a son, then you shall put him to death; but if it is a daughter, then she shall live." But the midwives feared God, and did not do as the king of Egypt had commanded them, but let the boys live. So the king of Egypt called for the midwives and said to them, "Why have you done this thing, and let the boys live?" The midwives said to Pharaoh, "Because the Hebrew women are not like the Egyptian women; for they are vigorous and give birth before the midwife can get to them." So God was good to the midwives, and the people multiplied, and became very mighty. And because the midwives feared God, He established households for them. Then Pharaoh commanded all his people, saying, "Every son who is born, you are to throw into the Nile, but every daughter, you are to keep alive." Ex. 1:15-22 (NASB)*

Let's break it down, shall we?

1. Pharaoh tells the midwives to kill the male Jewish babies.

2. The midwives disobey the demonic king's edict because they feared God.

3. God blesses the midwives who disobeyed the demented king.

Do you need another example of a rebel with a cause who blew off a bogus law that contradicted the word of God? If yes, then this is your lucky day. Check this out...

6:1 It pleased Darius to appoint 120 satraps over the kingdom, to be in charge of the whole kingdom, 2 and over them, three commissioners (of whom Daniel was one), so that these satraps would be accountable to them, and that the king would not suffer loss. 3 Then this Daniel began distinguishing himself]among the commissioners and satraps because he possessed an extraordinary spirit, and the king intended to appoint him over the entire kingdom. 4 Then the commissioners and satraps began trying to find a ground of accusation against Daniel regarding government affairs; but they could find no ground of accusation or evidence of corruption, because he was trustworthy, and no negligence or corruption was to be found in him. 5 Then these men said, "We will not find any ground of accusation against this Daniel unless we find it against him regarding the law of his God."

6 Then these commissioners and satraps came by agreement to the king and spoke to him as follows: "King Darius, live forever! 7 All the commissioners of the kingdom, the prefects and the satraps, the counselors and the governors, have consulted

Dear Christian: Your Fear is Full of Crap

together that the king should establish a statute and enforce an injunction that anyone who offers a prayer to any god or person besides you, O king, for thirty days, shall be thrown into the lions' den. 8 Now, O king, establish the injunction and sign the document so that it will not be changed, according to the law of the Medes and Persians, which may not be revoked." 9 Thereupon, King Darius signed the document, that is, the injunction.

10 Now when Daniel learned that the document was signed, he entered his house (and in his roof chamber he had windows open toward Jerusalem); and he continued kneeling on his knees three times a day, praying and offering praise before his God, just as he had been doing previously. 11 Then these men came by agreement and found Daniel offering a prayer and imploring favor before his God. 12 Then they approached and spoke before the king about the king's injunction: "Did you not sign an injunction that any person who offers a prayer to any god or person besides you, O king, for thirty days, is to be thrown into the lions' den?" The king replied, "The statement is true, according to the law of the Medes and Persians, which [j]may not be revoked." 13 Then they responded and spoke before the king, "Daniel, who is one of the [exiles from Judah, pays no attention to you, O king, or to the injunction which you signed, but keeps offering his prayer three times a day." Dan. 6:1-13 (NASB)

Here are my three takeaways from the above text.

1. The King commands everyone to pray to his ridiculous self and to no other God. (BTW, that clearly clashes with what the scripture states. The Bible frowns upon praying to heathen kings versus a Holy God. Google it if you don't believe me).

2. Daniel, unlike the Covid compliant pastors, did not obey such a goofy law.

3. Daniel openly defied the ridiculous new rule. He boldly and publicly prayed to the true God at his own digs with his windows fully opened so that everyone could see him kneeling towards Jerusalem and he did it three times a day in case his rat fink neighbors didn't see him the first two times.

Here's another delicious example of obeying God versus some created being who sports a plastic badge.

> *"By faith Moses, when he was born, was hidden for three months by his parents, because they saw he was a beautiful child; and they were not afraid of the king's edict." Heb. 11:23 (NASB)*

- Did you catch that? Moses' folks didn't move in fear and obey the king's ludicrous law.

- Oh, and guess what? God commended them for their act of civil disobedience by spotlighting them for all eternity in Hebrews chapter 11 also known as, "The Hall of Faith."

- #Boom.

Moving from Moe's mom and dad, let's look at another great example of not obeying unrighteous laws.

> *"1 Now after Jesus was born in Bethlehem of Judea in the days of Herod the king, behold, magi from the east arrived in Jerusalem, saying, 2 "Where is He who has been born King of the Jews? For we saw His star in the east and have come to worship Him." 3 When Herod the king heard this, he was troubled, and all Jerusalem with him. 4 And gath-*

ering together all the chief priests and scribes of the people, he inquired of them where the Messiah was to be born. 5 They said to him, "In Bethlehem of Judea; for this is what has been written by the prophet:

6 'And you, Bethlehem, land of Judah,

Are by no means least among the leaders of Judah;

For from you will come forth a Ruler

Who will shepherd My people Israel.'"

7 Then Herod secretly called for the magi and determined from them the exact time the star appeared. 8 And he sent them to Bethlehem and said, "Go and search carefully for the Child; and when you have found Him, report to me, so that I too may come and worship Him." 9 After hearing the king, they went on their way; and behold, the star, which they had seen in the east, went on ahead of them until it came to a stop over the place where the Child was to be found. 10 When they saw the star, they rejoiced exceedingly with great joy. 11 And after they came into the house, they saw the Child with His mother Mary; and they fell down and worshiped Him. Then they opened their treasures and presented to Him gifts of gold, frankincense, and myrrh. 12 And after being warned by God in a dream not to return to Herod, the magi left for their own country by another way." Matt. 2:1-12 (NASB)

Let's unpack this bad boy.

1. Herod wants the magi to give up the 411 where baby Jesus can be found.

2. God warns the magi in a dream to rebel against Herod.

3. The magi pony up and blew Herod's kingly request off.

And lastly, here's uno mas example of righteous rebellion exhibited by the apostle Paul when he got confronted
with an ungodly law.

> *"In Damascus the ethnarch under Aretas the king*
> *was guarding the city of the Damascenes in order*
> *to seize me, and I was let down in a basket through*
> *a window in the wall, and so escaped his hands."*
> *2Cor.11:32,33 (NASB)*

What do we have here little children? Well, three things
…

1. Bad dudes tried to arrest Paul for preaching.

2. Paul does some epic James Bond getaway stuff.

3. Paul, who crafted Romans 13, did not submit and
obey the ethnarch and his stupid desire to confine
Paul.

The End.

Culture Warrior Battle Notes

Chapter Nine: Jesus & Social Distancing

"The early church was married to poverty, prisons, and persecutions. Today, the church is married to prosperity, personality, and popularity."
– Leonard Ravenhill

Churches and pastors acted silly, or sad rather, during the bad cold of 2020-2021+.

They shut down their church because of unconstitutional and anti-Christian edicts.

They socially distance themselves from saints and sinners because it's now the "new normal".

Governors told them how they can meet and conduct ministry.

Pathetic. Truly, pathetic.

With that said, let's talk about the whole "social distancing" bag of hooey that we were sold. Would Jesus run from someone who had a contagious disease?

Exactly what would Jesus do? Well, let's go to the scripture, shall we?

8 When Jesus came down from the mountain, large crowds followed Him. 2 And a man with leprosy came to Him and bowed down before Him, and said, "Lord, if You are willing, You can make me clean." 3 Jesus reached out with His hand and touched him, saying, "I am willing; be cleansed." And immediately his leprosy was cleansed. 4 And Jesus *said to him, "See that you tell no one; but go, show yourself to the priest and present the offering that Moses commanded, as a testimony to them." Matt. 8:1-4 (NASB)

These four verses from Matthew's quill spotlight three aspects of biblical ministry that are evaporating, in many Churches, like a pack of smokes at an AA meeting.

What are they, you ask?

Well, I'm glad you inquired, you inquiring mind.

They are:

1. Jesus was a mountain man.

2. Jesus wasn't scared of lepers.

3. Jesus wasn't some little dandy that bragged about what He did.

Let's chip away at *numero uno*, shall we?

Jesus was a mountain man. I'm gonna take a rabbit trail for a sec but we'll quickly get to Jesus and social distancing. Y'all ready? Well, giddy up.

I'll never forget attending a pastor's retreat in Texas many moons ago where I was publicly chastised during a dinner for ordering one Coors Lite.

Dear Christian: Your Fear is Full of Crap

That's one ... Coors ... Lite.

Not twenty.

Not seven.

Not two.

Just one.

I was told by this minister that I was being a "bad witness" by drinking beer in public and that according to him, Jesus was angry with me.

What I found ironic was the fact that he was about two-hundred pounds overweight, had more chins than a Chinese phonebook and could barely walk across the restaurant parking lot because he was so out of shape.

Another thing I thought was a tad bit weird was him getting fussy about my one Silver Bullet when he had seventeen pieces of fried catfish and thirty-three hushpuppies. "Physician, heal thyself" seems a befitting verse for Mr. Busybody.

If Jesus were alive today and hanging out on a mountain top old chunky butt would be left in the dust because of his self-imposed obesity and rank inactivity.

Men should be hardy and able bodied, like Jesus.

Jesus often hung out in the mountains.

Back then, there were no ski lifts or helicopters to transport one to a summit. Jesus had to be physically fit to get to these high places that he loved to frequent.

When most people think of Jesus nowadays, they think of some pale-skinned indoor boy that hangs out with the Virgin Mary all the time talking about how mean the other boys are to him.

Most of the Christian art, which is total effeminate crap in my estimation, depicts Jesus as some squeamish, non-athletic, Boy George-type dreamy savior who walks around in a taupe *penoir* and sandals. In my mind's eye, I see the Son of Man more like a Bear Grylls, who has no problemo whatsoever traversing streams, bounding over boulders, scaling a rock face, or piloting a gruff skiff in rough seas.

Christian males, especially in big cities, wouldn't dare try to conquer a mountain because that would require sweat, getting dirty, possibly twisting an ankle or worse ... like wrecking their manicure they just got at Shambreeka's Nail Salon.

If you want your holy testosterone to kick in gents, get beyond the pavement, away from the lame and tame and interface with the wild just like Jesus did. It's magical. It's healthy. Be like Jesus and head often to the hills. Every time He retreated to the woods, He'd come back refreshed, filled with the Holy Ghost, and ready to stomp more demonic skulls.

Forgive that little rabbit trail.

Let's go back to Jesus and social distancing...

Unlike a lot of terrified pastors, during the pusillanimous plague, Jesus willingly interfaced with the forbidden lepers. Yes, leprosy is a contagion.

If you had leprosy back in JC's day, then guess what? Uber-religious people wouldn't go anywhere near you.

Not only did your ears, fingers, toes, nose, and penis fall off, you also didn't smell that hot and you had the added displeasure of lumps covering your noggin. In addition, to that humiliation you were banished to live in a Lepers Only subdivision that was about as appealing as watching Joe Biden and Nancy Pelosi dirty dance.

In other words, no one wanted their picture taken with you to share on their Instagram page if you were a leper.

Dear Christian: Your Fear is Full of Crap

Lepers were deemed "unclean" by Moses in Num. 5:1-4. Therefore, if you wanted to be considered Lysol-disinfected by The Law of Moses and respected by the pretty people of the Old Order you kept the heck away from the lepers and the leper colony.

Jesus shattered that rule.

Following the New Covenant law of love, Jesus healed the audacious leper whose faith dared him to approach the Son of God.

Oh, and by the way, Jesus could have healed the dude with His word alone (Luke 7:1-10) but He went a step further and touched him. That was completely unnecessary for Christ to render His supernatural power, but He did it anyway.

Please note: Jesus …

1. Wasn't wearing a dirty mask.

2. Didn't tell the sick brother to stay six feet away.

3. Didn't tell the leper to go home and watch Him preach via Facebook Live until he got better.

4. Get an anti-Hansen Disease shot.

5. Didn't furiously wash his hands like some deranged Howard Hughes after touching the leper.

6. Touched the grievously sick man that religious leaders avoided like a STD-riddled pirate hooker.

That's what Jesus would do.

Which means, I guess, that Pastor Jesus would've been fined and/or jailed if He was around during the mass delusional psychosis of 2020-2021+ because He clearly didn't obey the law of the land.

And finally, and I love this part, Jesus told the former leper, *"See that you tell no one; but go, show yourself to the priest and present the offering that Moses commanded, as a testimony to them."*

There are two things I dig about verse four of Matthew chapter eight:

1. Jesus said to tell no one.

2. Jesus sent the "unclean leper" to the priest for a little show-and-tell.

It takes a man to not brag about what they've done. Most pastors today would've dragged that leper around the planet showing off how God has used them to heal this poor guy. They'd put it on Facebook, call up Oprah, and try to get Netflix to do a documentary about their mighty healing ministry.

Jesus, on the other hand, said tell no one. Jesus, you see, wasn't some little fame-seeking Christian tinkerpot. The only person JC wanted him to tell was the priest who deemed lepers as unsavory compost that shouldn't be touched but rather left to rot.

Culture Warrior Battle Notes

Chapter Ten: 12 Days Of The Pandemic – The Lord Fauci Version
(To be sung to the tune of, The 12 Days of Christmas)

*"Preacher, keep your knees on the ground and your
eyes on the throne."*
– Leonard Ravenhill

On the 1st day of the pandemic Lord Fauci gave to me, a face mask to wear 'til 2033.

On the 2nd day of the pandemic Lord Fauci gave to me, 2 surgical gloves.

On the 3rd day of the pandemic Lord Fauci gave to me, 3 bald-faced lies.

On the 4th day of the pandemic Lord Fauci gave to me, 4 runny turds.

On the 5th day of the pandemic Lord Fauci gave to me, 5 Zoom meetings.

Doug Giles

On the 6th day of the pandemic Lord Fauci gave to me, 6 Psakis braying.

On the 7th day of the pandemic Lord Fauci gave to me, 7 lies a-spinnin'.

On the 8th day of the pandemic Lord Fauci gave to me, 8 more months of lockdowns.

On the 9th day of the pandemic Lord Fauci gave to me, 9 scientists prancing.

On the 10th day of the pandemic Lord Fauci gave to me, 10 anchors bloviating.

On the 11th day of the pandemic Lord Fauci gave to me, 11 neighbors spying.

On the 12th day of the pandemic Lord Fauci gave to me, 12 more dumb & dumbers.

Culture Warrior Battle Notes

Chapter Eleven: Anxiety Is A Sin. That Should Worry You.

*"There are three persons living in each of us: the one
we think we are, the one other people think we are,
and the one God knows we are."*
– Leonard Ravenhill

2020-2021+ saw a spike in stress, anxiety, depression, addiction, domestic violence, suicidal ideation which we are all traceable to the climate of fear stoked by public health authorities and the fake news spewers according to Dr. Mark McDonald. Big government and their lackeys in the media sold fear and America bought it – even Christians. Here's what Jesus had to say about the sin of living in fear. Enjoy.

> 25 *"For this reason I say to you, do not be worried about your life, as to what you will eat or what you will drink; nor for your body, as to what you will put on. Is life not more than food, and the body more than clothing? 26 Look at the birds of the sky, that they do not sow, nor reap, nor gather crops into barns, and yet your heavenly Father feeds them. Are you not much more important than they? 27 And which of you by worrying can add a single day to his life's span? 28 And why are you worried about clothing? Notice how the lilies of the*

field grow; they do not labor nor do they spin thread for cloth, 29 yet I say to you that not even Solomon in all his glory clothed himself like one of these. 30 But if God so clothes the grass of the field, which is alive today and tomorrow is thrown into the furnace, will He not much more clothe you? You of little faith! 31 Do not worry then, saying, 'What are we to eat?' or 'What are we to drink?' or 'What are we to wear for clothing?' 32 For the Gentiles eagerly seek all these things; for your heavenly Father knows that you need all these things. 33 But seek first His kingdom and His righteousness, and all these things will be provided to you.

34 "So do not worry about tomorrow; for tomorrow will worry about itself. Each day has enough trouble of its own. Matt. 6:25-34 (NASB)

I've spoken at, and have attended, many, many, "Christian Men's Conferences." Most, if not all of them, usually boil down to one message which is: "quit masturbating." Yep, that's what they all seem to deduce down to; namely, love God, love your family, and stop whipping the bishop.

Seldom, if ever, have I heard the pastors, who chair these "Men's Meetings," talk about the sin of worry which is a big sin in Jesus' eyes.

Matter of fact, in the aforementioned text, Jesus jackhammers those who wallow in worry because that vice eviscerates one's trust in the nature and character of God, the Father, and that ain't cool with Jesus, the Son.

When Jesus smelled worry, doubt, and fear in His boys, He fish-slapped that out of them, PDQ. To Jesus, worry was an egregious affront to the faithful love and care of the Father.

Jesus was not saddled with worry.

Why wasn't He?

Well, it was principally because He wasn't a tinkerpot and He knew and trusted His heavenly Father's rock-solid

Dear Christian: Your Fear is Full of Crap

dependability.

Worry is definitely not masculine.

Think of the pathetic and emasculated images that worry and anxiety spawn.

It's stuff like biting fingernails, chewing your lower lip, sweating like Adam Schiff at a Trump rally, fidgeting, tapping your feet and fingers nervously, jiggling your keys and change in your pocket while getting ready to bolt like a quail on point by a bird dog.

Jesus didn't roll like that. He was bold in the face of Cat5 hurricanes, lack of food, no place to live, going toe-to-toe with *el Diablo*, hostile mobs, cruel beatings, and ultimately His brutal death on a cross.

Worry was not a part and parcel of His holy repertoire, and He was not going to tolerate it in His disciples. It was a sin and when it manifested in His disciples, He rebuked it out of them.

Instead of truly believing and trusting in the provision and protection of God, nowadays Christian men pursue what they believe will secure them, i.e., material things, 401k's, tribulation shelters, mommy and daddy, and of course Visa, MasterCard, and American Express all the while numbing their anxieties with Xanax, Klonopin, Librium, Valium, and Ativan in order to offset their worries which the scripture calls the sin of unbelief.

Speaking of sin.

Much of the Church has a totemic view of vice.

The Catholics definitely do.

The Evangelicals do as well but we haven't organized them officially under such monikers such as "Mortal" and "Venial" sins.

Within the Medieval Church's definition of "The Seven Deadly Sins" worry and anxiety -- which the scripture deems and damns as unbelief -- isn't even mentioned. Hello.

So, why does worry get a pass from the Church and not from Christ?

I'll tell you why. It's because we all do it and worry doesn't have the scandalous "buzz" sins like lust and wrath gin up.

Jesus rebuked His boys and exhorted them away from sweating the necessities of life like food, drink, and clothing, which were hard to come by back then as there were few grocery stores, zero shopping malls, no Papa Johns, or Starbucks, and Evian wasn't even invented until the 20th century.

Christ's crowd were farmers and ranchers in an arid locale that could see brutal droughts and in the face of inclement conditions Jesus said, effectively, "don't sweat it... God's got your back ... He likes you better than birds and grass which are well taken care of and beautifully adorned by Him."

Jesus said your focus should not be on fretting about such things but on His kingdom concerns and He promised when your sights are locked-on to establish His will and way on the earth that God will float your boat.

Men, when they are worried, are refusing to trust God and thereby they let Him, their family, the church, and their nation down by curling up in the fetal position versus standing forthright, in faith, against everything Satan, life and a bad cold can toss at them.

Run from the sin of worry, my brothers.

Be bold.

Be strong and trust God in the face of adversity and watch your heavenly Father show Himself mighty on your behalf.

Dear Christian: Your Fear is Full of Crap

Culture Warrior Battle Notes

Chapter Twelve: Enlarged Through Distress

John the Baptist's training was in God's University of Silence. God takes all His great men there."
– Leonard Ravenhill

The years 2020 - 2021+ were devastating to millions of people.

Lots of stress, to say the least.

Lives and businesses were crushed.

Nefarious forces were afoot making peoples' lives a living hell.

Oddly enough, for me personally, those two plus years weren't nearly as bad as the crap I went through from 2016 through 2018. Those years stretched me like a bungee cord with a fat woman on the other end of it.

In 2016, Facebook began to shadowban posts from our wildly popular news portal, ClashDaily.com (270M page views). This cut our ad revenue in half. In 2017 the punks at Facebook aggressively started to block our Facebook page (2M followers with a page reach of 10-20M per week) which further crushed our bottom line. Which was a very nice bottom line. In October of 2018, Facebook banned me for life. Other ad sources jumped onto the woke wagon and greatly demonetized our website because we stump for a Judeo-Christian worldview, common sense, The Constitution, The Bill of Rights, and The Declaration of Independence and we do it with an irreverent sense of humor.

Everything me, my wife, and my business partners had worked our butts off for, and succeeded greatly at, was ... poof ... gone ... all because of our aversion to kowtowing to the big tech liberal thought police.

I thought I was going to ride this great news portal we'd created off into the sunset. I was wrong. We were crushed. To say those days were hectic is to greatly understate the pain and the unknowing of "what's next, Lord?"

Our lives were under stress. That sweet income was kaput.

However, through that epic stress, our faith grew greatly (James 1:2-6).

God came through in a powerful way, just as He promised (Ps. 37:25).

Like He promised, God did exceedingly and abundantly beyond all we could ask or imagine (Eph. 3:20,21).

The following sermon, based on Psalm 4:1, became very true to my life during that grueling spate of crap years. I held on to that verse and many others when we were getting the shiitake mushrooms kicked out of us. If you're going through a rough patch right now, I hope it ministers to you the way it did for me. My message is titled, Enlarged Through Distress. Enjoy.

> *"Hear me when I call, O God of my righteousness: thou hast enlarged me when I was in distress; have mercy upon me, and hear my prayer." Ps. 4:1 (KJV).*
> Check out how other translators render that verse ...
>
> *... When I call, answer me, O God of my righteousness: in*

Dear Christian: Your Fear is Full of Crap

pressure thou hast enlarged me; (DARBY)

... "Whenever I was in distress, you enlarged me." (TPT)

... Answer my prayers, O True God, the righteous, who makes me right. I was hopelessly surrounded, and You rescued me. Once again hear me; hide me in Your favor; bring victory in defeat and hope in hopelessness. (VOICE)

Focus on these goodies God gave David when David was going through life's woodchipper.

"Thou hast enlarged me when I was in distress."

"In pressure thou hast enlarged me."

"I was hopelessly surrounded, and You rescued me. Once again hear me; hide me in Your favor; bring victory in defeat and hope in hopelessness."

David said he grew through his pain and that God enlarged him and rescued him, bringing victory in defeat and hope in hopelessness, hiding David in His favor.

Growth through pain.

Imagine that.

A lot of Christians aspire to grow in their faith.

David's growth in God was preceded by this thing called "distress."

For those of you not hip to the word distress, it means extreme pain, a state of danger or desperate need. In other words, the crap hit the fan in David's life (many, many times) and yet, David grew.

It's a funny thing about crap. We've got a spot in our massive backyard that, for whatever reason, our dogs like to fertilize. That little patch of Bermuda that they regularly pop a squat on is taller and greener than the rest of the grass that surrounds it. Why is it more radiant and healthy? Well, aside from the sunshine and rain, the only difference between it and the other turf is it gets pooped and peed on a lot, as did David (metaphorically speaking, of course).

The reason David knew God so well was because he was constantly under attack either by God's people or God's enemies. You see, David actually needed God. David's life was one storm/battle after the other. If he wasn't dealing with external enemies he was dealing with his internal demons. David had a target on his back and the devil constantly tried to take him out. *Ergo*, David, unlike most Christians, clung to God for deliverance and not MasterCard, Visa, American Express, mommy or daddy, or prescription drugs.

Through all the BS David plowed through, he didn't just barely make it. He frickin' grew like a weed. He thrived. He experienced God on a level that most Christians never will because most of the church does everything in its power to avoid pain and stress. David embraced the pain, relied heavily on God, and came to know God's person and works in an amazing way that we're fortunate to behold, especially in the Psalms.

David says in Ps. 4:1 and in Ps. 119:67, 68, and 71 that the distress and affliction that he went through, some via the hand of others and some created by his own stupid mistakes enlarged him and schooled him into keeping God's word. Hello.

Check it out ...

> "Before I was afflicted I went astray, But now I keep Your word. You are good and You do good; Teach me Your statutes... It is good for me that I was afflicted, So that I may learn Your statutes." Ps. 119: 67,68, 71 (NASB)

Please note -- after the pain, at least in David's life, came holy growth and a more circumspect walk with God.

Dear Christian: Your Fear is Full of Crap

David said that the distress and affliction allowing God is "good" and "does good." Yes, little Dinky. David said God is and does good even when He allows for distress and affliction in our lives.

David, after getting jackhammered in life, didn't curse God.

He didn't join some radical anti-theistic Marxist cabal.

He didn't become some pouty-ass college dropout who gets a neck tattoo that says, "God sucks."

He didn't get on Instagram and start caterwauling, "why me, Lord?"

He had the maturity to roll with the punches and to understand that for God to grow us weird critters up and into something He's not ashamed of (Heb. 2:11) sometimes, oftentimes, He's gotta pinch our gelatinous and insidious flesh (Heb. 12:4-11).

I was ministering in Miami ten years ago and there was this beautiful young college girl who came up to me after I finished preaching and she was just weeping. Out of control type stuff. I asked her what's going on? What can I do for you? Through the phlegm and tears she said she was so mad at God. I asked her, why? She said why did God allow me to get an STD? A particularly dreadful STD, by the way. I asked her if she had been promiscuous or did this thing come out of nowhere and saddle her? She told us that she'd been kinda sleeping around and *blah blah blah*. Then I asked how in the world could she have the audacity to blame God for her horrid decisions that led to this wicked disease? She knew what she was doing was wrong and now it's God's fault she has a brutal gift that keeps on giving? That would be like me eating nothing but chicken fried steak, all day, every day for 40+ years, while drinking a gallon of vodka every night for 20 years and chain-smoking Camel no-filters for the last 30 years and then I blame God for me lying on my deathbed at 50.

David's distress and affliction didn't lead him to blame or

get bitter at God. It led him to personal growth and a closer relationship with his Creator and that's exactly how we should respond when life, for whatever reason, dropkicks us into left-field.

A few years ago, I contemplated taking Brazilian Jiu Jitsu lessons at the ripe old age of 55. Both my daughters are black-belts in BJJ. So, I asked them what would be the first thing I'd learn if I started training? Would I learn some intricate UFC submission moves? What about headbutting? Or how to eye-gouge? Or where to bite my opponent? Or hair-pulling? Or groin attacks and small joint manipulations?!? My girls were like, "Uh ... no dad. The first thing you'll learn is how to fall." How to fall? Who the heck wants to learn how to fall? That sounded about as fun as kissing my sister.

For the BJJ practitioner, their advantages are readily show-cased when the fight goes to the ground. In other words, get-ting knocked down ain't a bad thing at all. For the BJJ scrapper it's exactly where they want to go.

When David had life knock him to the ground, he too saw that as an advantageous place to be because he understood that lowly position is a place enlargement of his person and his work and a great place to know God more deeply and see Him work more dramatically.

Herewith, are seven little nuggets on how to steady oneself for growth in God and in life when (not if) you get kicked in the teeth by some bad crap.

> 1. Stay objective. David said in Ps. 42:5 (NASB), *"Why are you in despair, my soul? And why are you restless within me? Wait for God, for I will again praise Him For the help of His presence, my God."* I don't know if you caught this or not, but David is talking to David. David is taking an ob-jective stance against his subjective self. Effectively, Da-vid is telling himself to quit being a whiny wuss. David's talking himself up and out of his little slough of despond

Dear Christian: Your Fear is Full of Crap

he's mired in. Y'know … It's great to have friends and family for encouragement but we've gotta learn to do this trick all by our lonesome or we could be screwed. Stay focused after getting pummeled. If you're still breathing, there's still hope.

2. Don't freak out. Who wants to be remembered as the freakazoid who's known for panicking? Not me, *señorita*. When you act out of fear, that's when you make some mondo mistakes (Deut. 20:8). Remember when fear tries to take you over that God would never give you a spirit of fear but of power, love, and a sound mind (2Tim. 1:7). Satan breeds fear, not Jehovah.

3. Be careful how you "see." Can you see good in the bad? If you can, you're a rare monkey in these days of mass delusional psychotics. When Saul and Israel saw Goliath, they saw a giant that was too big to kill. When teenage David saw Goliath, he saw a giant that was too big to miss (1Sam. 17:45-47). How do you "see" your obstacles? Too big? Too scary? Or do you view your setbacks as mere speedbumps in light of your awesome God who's even more big and scary than anything life and Satan can toss at you?

4. Nut up. (Deut. 23:1-6) Speaking of speedbumps, American Christians flip out when they go over mole hills in the Garden of Eden. Gritty, we're not. We're missing a tad bit of the plucky spirit that the early church had. Getting knocked down is par for the Christian course. Get up. Dust yourself off. Now, move forward in faith.

5. Be better than the godless. (Matt. 6:25-33) Jesus said in Matt. 6:25-33 that the Christian should be distinct from the godless in that they do not share the unwashed masses mass delusional psychosis over food, clothing, and shelter because the believer understands that if God feeds little birds and dresses up flowers with useless beauty then He'll take care of His followers. Hello.

6. Say "whatever" when Satan spews fear, terror, dread, panic and "fake news" into your noggin about your fu-

ture (1Pet. 5:8). Satan's a liar who spawns fear and accuses Christians. Which means, duh, the Christian shouldn't believe him. Declare God's promises over your life and not Satan's doom and gloom BS. Defy *el Diablo*. Defy your enemies. Prove everyone wrong.

7. Fix what you can fix. Say stuff in your life is way out of control in regard to what you can throttle. You can't fix it. Mama can't fix it. Your buddies can't fix it, etc. If that's true, you can always go to work on yourself. You always have an open door to God. There's nothing keeping you from giving of your time, talent, and treasure. There's nothing keeping you from loving more, caring more and being available for whatever the hand of God needs doing. Unless you're dead, of course. Indeed, there's a ton of stuff you can do in the midst of junk you currently can't do anything about.

Lastly, the suckiest suckful suck years of 2016-2018 when we lost our business due to Herr Zuckerberg's fascistic edicts, were actually a Godsend. Now, looking back, I thank Him for allowing this pain to happen in my life because now, though not perfect, I'm in a way better spot in life now than I was back then.

> *Consider it a sheer gift, friends, when tests and challenges come at you from all sides. You know that under pressure, your faith-life is forced into the open and shows its true colors. So don't try to get out of anything prematurely. Let it do its work so you become mature and well-developed, not deficient in any way.*
>
> *If you don't know what you're doing, pray to the Father. He loves to help. You'll get his help, and won't be condescended to when you ask for it. Ask boldly, believingly, without a second thought. People who "worry their prayers" are like wind-whipped waves. Don't think you're going to get anything from the Master that way, adrift at sea, keeping all your options open. (James 1:2-8, MSG)*

Culture Warrior Battle Notes

Chapter Thirteen: Shout At The Devil

*"Satan fools and feigns, blows and bluffs, and we
so often take his threats to heart and forget the
"exceeding greatness of God's power to us."*
– Leonard Ravenhill

Can you imagine going to a sporting event, or a UFC fight, or a rock concert, or Trump Rally or a hilarious stand-up comedy show, and no one shouted?

I'm talking, zero loud voices. No laughter. No emotion. Just crickets while the team played, or when the duo scrapped, or the band performed, or the comedian made his hilarious observations. No shouts.

How weird would that be?

It would be like you were attending a Biden/Harris Rally or something equally strange.

It would be bizarre because you're expected to shout and scream in those venues. You're expected to express joy, act the fool, be free, support your team, or your fighter, or your band, or your favorite comedian with this thing called, "loud noises."

Matter of fact, they hand out noise makers, or at least sell them, at some sporting events.

When I used to watch the NFL, before they became completely hijacked by the United States of Liberal Acrimony, the Seattle Seahawks' fans were notorious for making so much noise the opposing team couldn't hear their quarterback call the snap. The Seahawk fans used their shout as a weapon to advance their teams agenda, namely whup the opposing team's backside.

Indeed, the attendees at those various events are expected to get rowdy. It's a given.

The few that don't scream and shout are the weirdos who aren't into the activity that, for whatever reason, they decided to attend but not enjoy.

Those types of peeps are called a veritable "ball and chain" or a "Debbie Downer." They suck the life out of your source of entertainment. They think they're more mature than you because they don't demonstratively emote via the shout.

The aforementioned entertainment sources love the shout but where is shouting frowned upon?

Well, one place is in the library, of course. God forbid making any noise in there.

Also, during a jury selection. The court has a zero-yapping tolerance.

One doesn't normally shout during a ballet, I hear. I wouldn't know because I have no desire to see people prance around or walk on their toes while Tchaikovsky's *Swan Lake* plays in the background.

Dear Christian: Your Fear is Full of Crap

I shouted once during a quiet moment at a Jars of Clay concert. I thought it was funny but the seven thousand Christians in attendance didn't. It's a preternatural feeling the thought of being murdered by seven thousand sassy believers because you caused a hiccup in their Friday night Contemporary Christian Concert experience.

Another spot where shouting rarely occurs and if it does happen, it is short lived or frowned upon by leaders and joyless people is in this place called the church.

Yep, when's the last time you got a group of Christians together and it was marked by triumphant shouting? That long, eh?

Most Christian meetings are denoted with cheesy religious platitudes, heavy doses of Christianese, weird Christian hugs, solemnity, sorrow, hopelessness, judgmentalism or just some good, old fashioned doom and gloom.

Triumphant shouting? Eh, not so much.

Churches aren't doing a lot of that anymore. Especially predominantly white churches. They've got no shout in them. They're the inhibited dance party. If they do have a shout in them you have to slowly coax it out, like a scared turtle, over a long period of time and assure them that Jesus is okay with them shouting in church, in prayer, and during Bible study.

You want me to prove to you that shouting is supposed to be standard trade for the private and corporate life of the Christian?

Alrighty, then. Check out Paul's Holy Spirit inspired exhortation in his letter to the Church in Ephesus.

Therefore be careful how you walk, not as unwise men but as wise, [making the most of your time, because the days are evil. So then do not be foolish, but understand what the will of the Lord is. And do not get drunk with wine, for that is dissipation, but be filled with the Spirit, speaking to one another in psalms and hymns and spiritual songs, singing and making melody with your heart to the Lord ... Eph. 5:15-19 (NASB)

Some of you are thinking that I'm cuckoo, and that chunk of text had *nada* to do with shouting. Hold on there, Dinky. Let me break it down for you. Are you ready? You are? Well, giddy up.

1. Paul says walk as wise men and not idiots.

2. Make the most of your time. Meaning, get off social media and cease binge watching shows *ad nauseum, ad infinitum.*

3. Know what God's will is for your life and quit being a dillweed.

4. Don't get drunk. Please note that Paul doesn't say, "Don't drink wine" but don't get drunk. If you do get drunk, repent, and carry on. Next time stop at two instead of ten. And remember there's no condemnation in Christ (Rom. 8:1).

5. Focus on being filled with the Spirit and not Mad Dog 2020.

6. Speak and sing the Psalms to one another, making melody with our heart to the Lord.

Dear Christian: Your Fear is Full of Crap

Point number six is what I want to focus on.

We're commanded, by inspiration of the Holy Spirit, via Paul's pen, to speak and sing the Psalms. Did you catch that? In case you didn't, here're six different English translations of Ephesians 5:19.

When you meet together, sing psalms, hymns, and spiritual songs, as you praise the Lord with all your heart. (CEV)

addressing one another in psalms and hymns and spiritual songs, singing and making melody to the Lord with your heart, (ESV)

Speaking unto yourselves in Psalms, and hymns, and spiritual songs, singing and making melody to the Lord in your hearts, (GNV)

by reciting psalms, hymns, and spiritual songs for your own good. Sing and make music to the Lord with your hearts. (GW)

Talk with each other much about the Lord, quoting psalms and hymns and singing sacred songs, making music in your hearts to the Lord. (TLB)

... Sing the Songs of David (NLV)

God wants us, when we gather together, to sing the Psalms.

God wants us to recite the Psalms.

God wants us to quote the Psalms.

God wants the Psalms to teach me and admonish me according to this verse ...

"Let the word of Christ richly dwell within you, with all wisdom teaching and admonishing one another with psalms and hymns and spiritual songs, singing with thankfulness in your hearts to God." Col. 3:16 (NASB)

Whatever is in those Psalms, God wants that holy mojo in me and you.

Guess what's in the Psalms, genteel Christian?

Well, for one thing, there's 109 imprecations in 150 Psalms but you wouldn't know it because politically correct hipster pastors avoid those texts like Trump would a Nancy Pelosi lingerie party.

Also, there's also a deep-seated, can't miss it, eschatology of victory, unmistakably woven into the Psalms but it's hard for evangelicals to see it because Rapture Fever causes spiritual blindness.

Also, and please, don't tell the Baptists, but there's a lot of dancing in the Psalms. Personally, I don't dance. Not because I think it's a sin but primarily because I once saw myself dancing in full length mirrors at a nightclub and that image scared me straight.

In addition to that incomplete list of what we're to take onboard via The Psalms, another thing that gets ignored in our Churches is the command to shout. Yep, there's a whole lotta shoutin' going down in The Psalms.

The word "shout" occurs 116 times in the Bible (NASB) with The Psalms sporting the lion's share of the shouts coming in at 27 references to making vehement outcries of animated courage, screams of determination, peals of thunderous unrestrained war cries and exuberant joy. Isaiah comes in second with 21 shouts in 66 chapters.

Oh, by the way, those exhortations for the believer to shout are not just in the Pentecostal Bible or the African

Dear Christian: Your Fear is Full of Crap

Americans' Bible. They're in your Catholic, Episcopalian, Methodist, Lutheran and believe it or not … your Baptist Bible. Yep, whatever your flavor of Christianity is, if you take your scripture straight like I do my root beer, you cannot deny that the admonition for the believer to worship God with shouting is profuse, especially within the Psalms, as well as the Old Testament and the New. It's commanded.

Here's how narrow, myopic, abecedarian, and daft pearl-clutching evangelicals have become with commanded Christian behavior.

The Bible says …

- Don't fornicate.

- Don't get drunk

- Don't commit adultery

- Don't watch Netflix

- Don't smoke the Devil's lettuce.

You know what else the Bible says, Miss Hoity Toity?

It says, *"shout unto God with a voice of triumph"* - Ps. 47:1 (KJV)

That's a command, not a suggestion.

The unique thing about the Psalms, which is the largest book in the Bible by the way, which also happens to be the church's prayer and song book (Hello), is that it was written by a bunch of warrior poets not weepy Christian dandies. It would be like having Joe Rogan, or Chris Kyle, or Ted Nugent, or Kid Rock, or Joan Jett, or James Hetfield write worship music instead of what's foisted upon us, namely, the ubiquitous quasi-male, evangelical, rouged and giddy, American Idol wannabe, "worship" leader.

David wrote the majority of these fire-breathing verbal offerings. Moses and Asaph have a few in there as well. But all the dudes who wrote this tome were familiar with and participants in war and they knew God as an Exodus 15:3 God of War.

The gents who penned these poems didn't sit around Starbucks in Nashville with Frappuccinos scribbling song ideas just to make a Christian hit record that would impress their gullible goggle-eyed girlfriend they're fornicating with.

Most of these songs were written before, during or after some bloody battle. Thus, the shout of faith, the shout for help and the shout of victory made sense and was very *apropos*.

The reason there's very little shouting in Christian circles is because a lot of Christians are wussies and they're hiding from the Devil instead of resisting him.

Yep, the reason there's no shouting in Church today is because Christians are not going into battle.

If you were going into battle, or if you are currently embroiled in one, or you have just returned from an epic throwdown, shouting would be easy for you. It makes sense. That's what warriors do. They shout.

Again, a lot of the Psalmist's shouts were in bad situations, or prior to an enemy engagement, or after a massive butt-kicking of the enemies of God. Church to them resembled a football locker room pep talk or some battlefield lets-get-psyched-up-rally.

Dear Christian: Your Fear is Full of Crap

From The Psalms the Christian is admonished to …

1. Shout to God before you engage the enemy.

2. Shout to God for help before the temptation to sin.

3. Shout to God once you're in the fire fight.

4. Shout praises to Him for all victories, small and large.

Here's a short list of the power of a shout throughout scripture.

For those unfamiliar with what a shout is, Webster's defines it as: "A vehement and sudden outcry, expressing joy, exultation, animated courage, or other emotion."

Look what God did when His people let a shout rip.

- The Walls of Jericho were brought down with a shout. (Josh. 6:5)

- After David killed Goliath Israel shouted as pursued and overtook the Philistines. (1Sam. 17:52)

- The people of God shouted when the temple was restored. (Ezra 3:11-13)

- He will yet fill your mouth with laughter And your lips with shouting. (Job 8:21)

- For His anger is but for a moment, His favor is for a lifetime; Weeping may last for the night, But a shout of joy *comes* in the morning (Ps. 30:5)

- Let them shout for joy and rejoice ...; And let them say continually, "The Lord be magnified, Who delights in the prosperity of His servant." (Ps. 35:27)

- The sound of joyful shouting and salvation is in the tents of the righteous; (Ps. 118:15)

- When it goes well with the righteous, the city rejoices, And when the wicked perish, there is joyful shouting. (Prov. 11:10)

- Behold, My servants will shout joyfully with a glad heart ... God shouts over you ... (Isa. 65:14)

- The Lord your God is in your midst, A victorious warrior. He will exult over you with joy, He will be quiet in His love, He will rejoice over you with shouts of joy. (Zeph. 3:17)

If you want to get Jesus' attention, try shouting. Check this out ...

On the next day, when they came down from the mountain, a large crowd met Him. And a man from the crowd shouted, saying, "Teacher, I beg You to look at my son, for he is my only boy, and a spirit seizes him, and he suddenly screams, and it throws him into a convulsion with foaming at the mouth; and only with difficulty does it leave him, mauling him as it leaves. I begged Your disciples to cast it out, and they could not." And Jesus answered and said, "You unbelieving and perverted generation, how long shall I be with you and put up with you? Bring your son here." While he was still approaching, the demon slammed him to the ground and

Dear Christian: Your Fear is Full of Crap

threw him into a convulsion. But Jesus rebuked the unclean spirit, and healed the boy and gave him back to his father. And they were all amazed at the greatness of God. Luke 9: 37-43 (NASB)

If you hate shouting, you'll hate the book of Revelation. Loud voice(s) are recognized twenty-one times in The Apocalyspe. That's half of the loud voices in the New Testament and 1/3rd of the loud voices in the whole of the scripture.

Here's a worship service according to Psalm 149 (NASB). Compare this to your church's.

1 Praise ye the Lord. Sing unto the Lord a new song, and his praise in the congregation of saints.

2 Let Israel rejoice in him that made him: let the children of Zion be joyful in their King.

3 Let them praise his name in the dance: let them sing praises unto him with the timbrel and harp.

4 For the Lord taketh pleasure in his people: he will beautify the meek with salvation.

5 Let the saints be joyful in glory: let them sing aloud upon their beds.

6 Let the high praises of God be in their mouth, and a two-edged sword in their hand;

7 To execute vengeance upon the heathen, and punishments upon the people;

8 To bind their kings with chains, and their nobles with fetters of iron;

9 To execute upon them the judgment written: this honour have all his saints. Praise ye the Lord.

If you're SHOUTING, you're alive in God, protected, and blessed. That sounds good to me.

Finally, this is very interesting and cool. In Numbers 23, Balak wants Balaam to curse/damn the people of God and all Balaam does, heretofore, is bless them, much to the chagrin of Balak. So, Balaam responds to Balak …

> … *Rise up, Balak, and hear; hearken unto me, thou son of Zippor:*
>
> *God is not a man, that he should lie; neither the son of man, that he should repent: hath he said, and shall he not do it? or hath he spoken, and shall he not make it good?*
>
> *Behold, I have received commandment to bless: and he hath blessed; and I cannot reverse it.*
>
> *He hath not beheld iniquity in Jacob, neither hath he seen perverseness in Israel: the Lord his God is with him, and the shout of a king is among them. Num. 23:18-21 (NASB)*

Did you catch that? The people of God could not be cursed for the shout of the king is among them.

If you want your current crappy situation to change – I'd start shouting.

Dear Christian: Your Fear is Full of Crap

Culture Warrior Battle Notes

Chapter Fourteen: The "F" Word

"My goal is GOD HIMSELF. Not joy, not peace, not even blessing but HIMSELF...my GOD."
– Leonard Ravenhill

Relax, sister. I'm not talking about that "F" word. Get your mind out of the gutter. There are words that start with "F" other than "fear" and "Fauci," you know.

The "F" word that I'm concerned with in this chapter is -- drum roll, please -- *faith*.

Faith is the key to keep you going when you begin to plow through "hell."

Faith crushes doubts, fears, demons, circumstances, and the silliness that seeks to hamstring the warrior in his pursuit of his Holy Grail. So, how do we get the butt-kickin' and trial-stompin' faith that causes one to believe in hope against hope? That question is answered by Paul in Romans 10:17 …

"So faith comes from hearing, and hearing by the word of Christ." Rom. 10:17 (NASB)

Sounds easy, eh?

Faith comes by hearing and hearing the Word of God.

Hmmm ...

All we have to do is hear the Word of God?

Sounds like a piece of cake, doesn't it?

Just hearing the Word?

That's easy, eh?

Paul has got to mean something other than audibly receiving the spoken Word because I know a stack of people who have heard the Word of God preached and sung for the last fifteen Olympics who lose their faith once life starts to fish-slap the snot out of them.

They do not manifest faith; they instead manifest fear and proceed to coil up in the fetal position and let demons use them as a doormat. It's as if they heard the Word but *didn't* hear it. Are you hearing what I'm saying?

They're kind of like me when my wife tells me something while I'm smoking a cigar and watching a Craig Boddington African hunting movie. I hear her, but I'm not listening to her.

So how do we *hear* the Word of God when we are hearing the Word of God? I'll touch on that later. For now, I'd like to talk about *what* we are to hear and then a little on *how* we are to hear.

If you're going to live a life of faith, where you rule and your bad cold trial drools, then you had better have your head under the spout where the glory comes out.

A hunger and thirst for the Word of God is a must if you wish to live a life of overcoming faith. It is a must. It is not an option. The Apostle Paul says faith comes from this fountain. Faith doesn't come from just feeling positive because an intense trial will melt away all of your upbeat feelings quicker than a mid-August South Florida sun will liquefy an overly made-up chick's Cover Girl face paint.

Dear Christian: Your Fear is Full of Crap

Yep, faith is not about your being positive and chipper like some dippy cheerleader. It's deeper than that. It is about you, not your wife, not your mommy or your grandmother, but you, having a substantial, subterranean, spiritual river of the Word of God flowing through your soul that feeds and fuels your spirit when you bump up against the forces of hell.

Check it out.

A heart (not just a head) full of the Word of God is a heart that is full of faith in God. Which means, Dinky, you have got to start devouring the scripture if you want to walk in the power of His Spirit and not in fear. You must stockpile the Word of God the same way Elaine Benes hoarded contraceptives on *Seinfeld*.

This is easy to do.

At least it used to be easy to do when our nation could actually read. I'm going to go out on a limb here and guess that since you have made it to this point in the book, you're probably able to read, at least at the third-grade level at which I write. Congrats, *Slumdog Millionaire*! Since you are reading these words right now, you're one of the lucky one-out-of-four that actually made it through public school with the ability to read, right?

Now since it is established that you can read, let me ask thou this: are you reading the Bible? I'm talking from stem to stern, from soup to nuts, from Adam to the Anti-Christ, both widely and deeply?

Huh?

If not, you're not serious yet about plowing through your private hell when it comes.

This is where a good chunk of the Church lives. They're not serious about being a holy warrior in life. They would love to be champions. They crave it, but they won't dig deep into the scripture, do their due diligence, and mine the principles and patterns inherent within the Bible which make them players when pain and problems arise.

Yes, these dreamers want victory but they're unwilling to do the hard work of stashing the Scripture in their hearts and souls. (Prov. 13:4.) The Word of God, according to the lame wussies, is just so tedious, taxing, time-consuming, and other troubling words that begin with a "T".

Frankly, I am amazed at the biblical illiteracy amongst Christians nowadays. It is rank. When I ask your typical Christian to rattle off the Ten Commandments, they recite to me AA's Twelve Steps.

If you want to be a mediocre Christian toad, then not having a substantial battery of Bible knowledge is groovy. Go for it. Let us know how it goes for you.

However, should you be the kind of person who wants to milk the highs and lows of life for all the experiences and excitements of a summit or plummet, God-honoring existence, then you need the Word of God in you more than Nancy Pelosi needs a lifetime supply of Botox and Fixodent.

Therefore (man, am I belaboring this point), if you want to be the fire walker instead of the little weenie wonk who gets steamrolled by life's hiccups or sidelined by some punk demon, then you, *mi amigo*, had better get a Bible you can read and begin devouring it PDQ.

Yes, since you have decided to throttle threats and bounce back when you have been crushed, you need the Word of God's principles, lessons, revelations, and narratives shooting through your system and formulating your attitudes and actions so that Satan will not hand you your arse when the trial comes.

For the word of God is living and active and sharper than any two-edged sword, and piercing as far as the division of soul and spirit, of both joints and marrow, and able to judge the thoughts and intentions of the heart.

Dear Christian: Your Fear is Full of Crap

And there is no creature hidden from His sight, but all things are open and laid bare to the eyes of Him with whom we have to do. Heb. 4:12-13 (NASB)

God's Word is not normal. His book has a freaky anointing built into it. God's Word is commanding. Think about it. By His *Word* the heavens were created. By Jesus' *Word* demons were exorcised, sick people healed, the dead were raised, cussing fishermen were called to holy service, and by His *Word* the Godhead states the obedient will triumph.

The Word of God has a punch to it that being Tony Robbins-upbeat cannot and does not deliver.

Oprah's little ditties don't have the *dunamis* that Jehovah's *verbum* does.

2 Grace and peace be multiplied to you in the knowledge of God and of Jesus our Lord, 3 for His divine power has granted to us everything pertaining to life and godliness, through the true knowledge of Him who called us by His own glory and excellence. 4 Through these He has granted to us His precious and magnificent promises, so that by them you may become partakers of the divine nature, having escaped the corruption that is in the world on account of lust. 2Pet. 1:2-4 (NASB)

Peter said that the promises of God, contained in the Scripture, are precious and magnificent and are given to us -- hello, Church -- for life and godliness. Yes, they help you with life and being godly. They will even cause nasty sin-riddled dorks like us to partake, in a limited way, of God's divine nature. That's whacked, folks.

Now, when Pete used the word "precious," he didn't mean they are sweet, dainty, and *aw shucks* cute, but precious as incredibly valuable in saving your backside and transforming your gross ordeal into a soul enlarging opportunity. Yep, the Word of God, in the power-over-problems sense of the word, is valued like gold, or platinum, or diamonds, or rubies, or pre-WWII English double rifles, or British-made bolt action rifles from the early part of the twentieth century, or ...

Sorry, I kind of went off track there.

Anyway, the Word of God is indispensable to your standing in faith. It is gold, baby, pure gold when you are going through hell.

With the Word of God your mind is renewed to His way (Rom. 12:1-2), His reality, His patterns and principles, which are *muy importante* because the ways in which we think are usually completely catawampus to the way God thinks when things begin to stink. Therefore, you must know it, or you will blow it.

And yes, I'm talking to you.

YOU must know the Scripture like YOU know the back of YOUR hand because YOUR carnal mind, YOUR natural thoughts in collusion with the powers of darkness are going to flood YOUR gray matter with all manner of doubts as to why YOU should not believe when YOU should.

Did you notice how I capitalized "you" and "your"?

You did?

That was me shouting at you in a high pitched and angry Nepalese accent attempting to emphasize that it's *your* job to know the Word of God like a mother orangutan knows the top of her bald-headed babies' noggins.

As you build your Bible knowledge stockade, you will quickly come to learn that when the shizzle hits the fan there is not a situation that you will be faced with that the Word of God doesn't speak to directly -- or indirectly -- via its principles and patterns. This reservoir of revelation will afford you the wisdom and power to stay afloat once you begin to surf Hades' waves. Without it, you're done.

For example:

Dear Christian: Your Fear is Full of Crap

Say you're going broke right now during this government-spawned recession from hell and yet you refuse to look to Biden or your mama to bail you out. Here are a few promises, just a few, that God gives to the faithful once they start going through a financial crap storm. With just the following four nuggets you can begin to get your soul built back up with knowledge and trust, grounded in the authority of the Scripture, that your rich Father, i.e., God, is not going to leave you schlepping around with a "Will work for beer" sign.

> *"And my God will supply all your needs according to His riches in glory in Christ Jesus" Phil. 4:19 (NASB).*

Paul said, *"My God will supply all your needs."* All of them. Not Biden. Not VISA. Not your mommy. Not some high interest loan shark, but God, Sling Blade. He will float your boat if you are obedient. No matter how rank the day, God has forsworn to support those who are about His business.

The $64,000 question is: Are you on the right side of God's business? If you are, then you need to quit freaking out about your finances. Run this verse about thirty times through your head and then shout it out at the top of your lungs that your God will meet your needs according to His riches in Christ Jesus. Now get off your butt and in faith, go get a job. Let this day be the last day you look to mama and MasterCard. Take a walk on the wild side of faith for your finances.

Here are three more chunks of holy cordite to load your soul with:

> *For the LORD your God has blessed you in all that you have done; He has known your wanderings through*

this great wilderness . These forty years the LORD your God has been with you; you have not lacked a thing. Deut. 2:7 (NASB)

For the LORD your God is bringing you into a good land, a land of brooks of water, of fountains and springs, flowing forth in valleys and hills; a land of wheat and barley, of vines and fig trees and pomegranates, a land of olive oil and honey; a land where you will eat food without scarcity, in which you will not lack anything; a land whose stones are iron, and out of whose hills you can dig copper. When you have eaten and are satisfied, you shall bless the LORD your God for the good land which He has given you. Deut. 8:7-10 (NASB)

The young lions do lack and suffer hunger; but they who seek the LORD shall not be in want of any good thing. Ps. 34:10 (NASB)

My wife and I raised our two daughters in Miami, Florida, one of the most beautiful, yet perverted places on the planet. I both loved it and hated it. I loved it for the lifestyle it afforded us. We loved the water and the weather. I hated it because that place is a veritable east coast Sin City, with higher humidity.

When we moved there, several people told us that we were insane to bring our two beautiful babies to such a morally vacuous place, and I, in part, sort of agreed with them. If my wife and I were faithless, cross-eyed, spiritual dill weeds who didn't have a stranglehold on the promises of God for our children, then, no doubt, our kids probably would be vexed by Miami's Vice.

But seeing that we are not faithless, cross-eyed, spiritual dill weeds (I might be other things, but not that), but rather a *contra mundus* couple who have an entire litany of Scriptures memorized and taken to heart, which God gives to obedient parents regarding the preservation and blessing upon their offspring, we have not sweated their upbringing in this licentious locale. And you know what? The Word of God worked -- imagine that! -- and our gorgeous girls are now righteous and rowdy women who never became a part of the local teen fart cloud.

In this secularized, sin-baptized *milieu,* you need faith to raise your kids in such a smut-filled environment. If you are a half decent parent, then I know you're groping for some promises that your children won't turn into Instagram prostitutes once they turn thirteen, right?

Parental units, you want the promises of God that your kids will be protected in this hellish culture and that your household will be uniquely blessed. If that's you, mom and dad, then check these bad boys out:

> *Praise the LORD! How blessed is the man who fears the LORD, who greatly delights in "His commandments. His descendants will be mighty on earth; the generation of the upright will be blessed. Wealth and riches are in his house, and his righteousness endures forever." Ps. 112:1-3 (NASB)*
>
> *"No evil will befall you, nor will any plague come near your tent." Ps. 91:10 (NASB)*
>
> *"He will bless those who fear the LORD, the small together with the great. May the LORD give you increase, you and your children." Ps. 115:13-14 (NASB)*
>
> *"The house of the wicked will be destroyed, but the tent of the upright will flourish." Prov. 14:11 (NASB)*

How about if the trial that you are facing relates to an illness, or a disease? As a realist, I'm all about going to the doctor. At the same time God, the Great Physician, has allotted to us promises for our infirmities.

Will everyone get miraculously healed if sick?

No.

Do I know why? That would be no, to the tenth power. Does that dissuade me from believing that Christ can and does heal? Nope.

I will always believe for divine help if my health goes south. Which, thanks be to God, it hasn't, and I have had great health for the last forty-nine years.

Try these mamas out.

> *Bless the LORD, O my soul, and all that is within me, bless His holy name. Bless the LORD, O my soul, and forget none of His benefits; Who pardons all your iniquities, who heals all your diseases; Who redeems your life from the pit, who crowns you with lovingkindness and compassion; Who satisfies your years with good things, so that your youth is renewed like the eagle. Ps. 103:1-5 (NASB)*

> *When evening came, they brought to Him many who were demon-possessed; and He cast out the spirits with a word, and healed all who were ill. This was to fulfill what was spoken through Isaiah the prophet: "HE HIMSELF TOOK OUR INFIRMITIES AND CARRIED AWAY OUR DISEASES." Matt. 8:16-17 (NASB)*

> *For you have made the LORD, my refuge, even the Most High, your dwelling place. No evil will befall you, nor will any plague come near your tent. For He will give His angels charge concerning you, to guard you in all your ways. They will bear you up in their hands, that you do not strike your foot against a stone. You will tread upon the lion and cobra, the young lion and the serpent you will trample down. Because he has loved Me, therefore I will deliver him; I will set him securely on high, because he has known My name. He will call upon Me, and I will answer him; I will be with him in trouble; I will rescue him and honor him. With a long life I will satisfy him and let him see My salvation. Ps. 91:9-16 (NASB)*

What if sin is getting the best of you and you're sick of being a slave to a certain vice? Slip on these PJ's before you capitulate to the flesh and live a life of quiet desperation:

Dear Christian: Your Fear is Full of Crap

"No temptation has overtaken you but such as is common to man; and God is faithful, who will not allow you to be tempted beyond what you are able, but with the temptation will provide the way of escape also, so that you will be able to endure it." 1Cor. 10:13 (NASB)

"For whatever is born of God overcomes the world; and this is the victory that has overcome the world— our faith." 1Jn. 5:4 (NASB)

"No weapon that is formed against you will prosper; and every tongue that accuses you in judgment you will condemn. This is the heritage of the servants of the LORD, and their vindication is from Me, declares the LORD." Isa. 54:17 (NASB)

"For sin shall not be master over you, for you are not under law, but under grace." Rom. 6:14 (NASB)

"What then shall we say to these things? If God is for us, who is against us? He who did not spare His own Son, but delivered Him up for us all, how will He not also with Him freely give us all things? Who will bring a charge against God's elect? God is the one who justifies; who is the one who condemns? Christ Jesus is He who died, yes, rather who was raised, who is at the right hand of God, who also intercedes for us. Who will separate us from the love of Christ? Will tribulation, or distress, or persecution, or famine, or nakedness, or peril, or sword? Just as it is written, 'FOR YOUR SAKE WE ARE BEING PUT TO DEATH ALL DAY LONG; WE WERE CONSIDERED AS SHEEP TO BE SLAUGHTERED.' But in all these things we overwhelmingly conquer through Him who loved us." Rom. 8:31-37 (NASB)

"What about if you have blown it severely and you're wondering if God will forgive or ever use you again? Slip these goodies into your psyche: Therefore there is now no condemnation for those who are in Christ Jesus. For the law of the Spirit of life in Christ Jesus has set you free from the law of sin and of death." Rom.

8:1-2 (NASB)

"If we confess our sins, He is faithful and righteous to forgive us our sins and to cleanse us from all unrighteousness." 1John. 1:9 (NASB)

"Therefore, confess your sins to one another, and pray for one another so that you may be healed. The effective prayer of a righteous man can accomplish much." James 5:16 (NASB)

Be gracious to me, O God, according to Your lovingkindness; according to the greatness of Your compassion blot out my transgressions. Wash me thoroughly from my iniquity and cleanse me from my sin. For I know my transgressions, and my sin is ever before me. Against You, You only, I have sinned and done what is evil in Your sight, so that You are justified when You speak and blameless when You judge. Behold, I was brought forth in iniquity, and in sin my mother conceived me. Behold, You desire truth in the innermost being, and in the hidden part You will make me know wisdom. Purify me with hyssop, and I shall be clean; wash me, and I shall be whiter than snow. Make me to hear joy and gladness, let the bones which You have broken rejoice. Hide Your face from my sins and blot out all my iniquities. Create in me a clean heart, O God, and renew a steadfast spirit within me. Do not cast me away from Your presence and do not take Your Holy Spirit from me. Restore to me the joy of Your salvation and sustain me with a willing spirit. Then I will teach transgressors Your ways, and sinners will be converted to You." Ps. 51:1-13 (NASB)

The aforementioned are just a smidgen; I said a smidgen, an infinitesimal fraction, a wee little taste-test of the good love God promises His people through His Word. If you do not have these deep within your soul, then like I said, when hell comes -- and it will -- Satan will put on his steel-toed combat boots and proceed to kick the stuffing out of you.

Guaranteed.

Dear Christian: Your Fear is Full of Crap

One of the greatest covenantal lists of positive perks the obedient believer needs to have in his head when he starts to go through hell is spelled out in OMG clarity in Deuteronomy 28:1-14 *(NASB)*:

1 Now it shall be, if you diligently obey the LORD your God, being careful to do all His commandments which I command you today, the LORD your God will set you high above all the nations of the earth.

2 All these blessings will come upon you and overtake you if you obey the LORD your God:

3 Blessed shall you be in the city, and blessed shall you be in the country.

4 Blessed shall be the offspring of your body and the produce of your ground and the offspring of your beasts, the increase of your herd and the young of your flock.

5 Blessed shall be your basket and your kneading bowl.

6 Blessed shall you be when you come in, and blessed shall you be when you go out.

7 The LORD shall cause your enemies who rise up against you to be defeated before you; they will come out against you one way and will flee before you seven ways.

8 The LORD will command the blessing upon you in your barns and in all that you put your hand to, and He will bless you in the land which the LORD your God gives you.

9 The LORD will establish you as a holy people to himself, as He swore to you, if you keep the commandments of the LORD your God and walk in His ways.

10 So all the peoples of the earth will see that you are called by the name of the LORD, and they will be afraid of you.

11 The LORD will make you abound in prosperity, in

the offspring of your body and in the offspring of your beast and in the produce of your ground, in the land which the LORD swore to your fathers to give you.

12 The LORD will open for you His good storehouse, the heavens, to give rain to your land in its season and to bless all the work of your hand; and you shall lend to many nations, but you shall not borrow.

13 The LORD will make you the head and not the tail, and you only will be above, and you will not be underneath, if you listen to the commandments of the LORD your God, which I charge you today, to observe them carefully, 14 and do not turn aside from any of the words which I command you today, to the right or to the left, to go after other gods to serve them.

It is important to have this spiritual ammo within your soul when the storms of life begin to batter you. When you have the Word of God dwelling in you richly, whatever the adverse and tense situation you are currently being boiled in, the Word of God, united with faith, will cause you to overcome when the crud comes. When our minds are renewed with the Word of God and we actually believe His reality versus the slop we're being saddled with, such trust will cause us to take on a posture of defiance in the most difficult of circumstances.

Life and death, according to Solomon, are in the power of the tongue. (Prov.18:21) I don't know about you, but when I am getting my physical ears boxed, I want my spiritual ears hearing His words of wisdom and faith instead of the world's stupidity and unbelief that often spawns from even the most well-meaning humanoids.

Having now lightly covered the importance of the Scripture when you begin to scrap in the pit of life, I wanna address *how* we can hear the Word of God *when* we hear it. The writer of Hebrews said that people could read and hear the Word of God and yet not profit from it.

Dear Christian: Your Fear is Full of Crap

Therefore, let us fear lest, while a promise remains of entering His rest, any one of you may seem to have come short of it. For indeed we have had good news preached to us, just as they also; but the word they heard did not profit them, because it was not united by faith in those who heard. Heb. 4:1-2 (NASB)

The writer of Hebrews warns New Testament Christians of the danger of hearing the Word, as Israel did in the wilderness, and not profit from it because of unbelief.

I like profit.

Profit is good.

I have never profited from anything and thought,

"Yecch ... that sucked!"

Yes, indeed, I want to hear the Word of God in the way in which it was intended to be heard with the resultant effect being a solid trust in God that inspires faith, encourages me to take risks, and makes me stand for that which is holy, just, and good when others are caving in all around me.

So, how do we hear when we are hearing?

First of all, you have to have a sincere heart, or the Word of God will bounce off you like a Slim Fast shake off a fat sister's palette. When one comes to the Word of God, in private study or in public worship, you must come humbly, hungry, honest, and open if you want to profit from the scripture.

If you're a know-it-all dork or a selfish me-monkey who has zero intention of repenting, or you are more famished for what Madison Avenue has for you than *Yahweh,* then more than likely the Word of God is going to come off as about as inspiring as the operation handbook for a doorknob. Therefore, God's not going to wow you with revelation or give you what He gave Abraham; you don't give a crap about Him, so why should God give a crap about you? He's not going to reveal Himself to you, or infuse you with hell defying, Hebrews 11 kind of faith with your kind of attitude. Jesus does not throw His pearls to swine (Matthew 7:6) and that's what you are if you approach God in such a *laissez faire* way ... a pig.

A mud lovin' Wilbur.

The person who comes to God's Word with a sincere heart seeking to grow thereby is the one to whom God will make that ink on a page become the living and dynamic Word of Life.

It's that simple.

A right heart opens the spiritual ear causing the owner of that sincere heart to, by faith....

Stand and not fall.

See the unseen.

Walk on the path of obedience instead of rebellion.

Be courageous and not cowardly.

Speak His Word and not your fear.

Work His works instead of quit and give up.

Fight and not become passive.

Inherit the promises versus the blunt end of hell's pool cue.

9 The one who has ears, let him hear." Matt. 13:9 (NASB)

Culture Warrior Battle Notes

Chapter Fifteen: Jesus Promised Problems

"How can you pull down strongholds of Satan if you don't even have the strength to turn off your TV?"
– Leonard Ravenhill

"God whispers to us in our pleasures, speaks to us in our conscience, but shouts in our pains: It is His megaphone to rouse a deaf world." – C.S. Lewis

> *These words I speak to you are not incidental additions to your life, homeowner improvements to your standard of living. They are foundational words, words to build a life on. If you work these words into your life, you are like a smart carpenter who built his house on solid rock. Rain poured down, the river flooded, a tornado hit— but nothing moved that house. It was fixed to the rock. But if you just use my words in Bible studies and don't work them into your life, you are like a stupid carpenter who built his house on the sandy beach. When a storm rolled in and the waves came up, it collapsed like a house of cards. (Matt. 7:24-27, MSG)*

In Jesus' first meet-and-greet He branded His believers, right off the bat, with the promise of pain. Storms for everyone. We will all go through hell. Not literal hell, but pain-in-the-butt hell. I know this information is wedging sideways with some. They're thinking ...

Storms?

At the hand of God?

WTH?

No, thank you.

That ain't right.

My grinning, cheesy, over-moussed minister who puts the "gel" in evangelical never told me that smack.

"God would never allow His precious ones to go through a hellacious storm, would He? I understand God giving the blunt end of the pool cue to the overtly impious, rebellious rats that whizz on His commandments, but Christians too? What kind of thank you is that for following His commands and listening to Christian rock? That's no way to treat your friends, Yahweh. No wonder not too many people are lining up to follow You nowadays," thus saith the self-obsessed, me-monkey kind of Christian.

Now, contrary to the American Crapola Gospel peddled by tawdry pseudo-Christian hucksters on YouTube, Jesus promised not only puppy dogs and candy canes for Christians, but He also promised life-razing storms.

Yeah ... He assured us of bad stuff.

Matter of fact, when the Son of God chose an image to give the sense of what He was forewarning His followers about, He used three metaphors so that it would be unmistakable what kind of bovine scat they should brace for—namely, rains, floods, and winds that are so violent that if our "house" isn't built well, well ... we're screwed.

Now, most of us would like to think that the righteous would get a reprieve from pain, but to do so will make us as

Dear Christian: Your Fear is Full of Crap

wrong as Hunter Biden is shady and bleary-eyed.

I've spent 50+ years of my life in two deadly storm-riddled area codes -- the 806 and the 305 -- West Texas and South Florida, respectively. In West Texas, there were tornadoes. In South Florida, it's hurricanes. Having experienced both these death-dealers, all I've got to say is ... I prefer a hurricane to a tornado.

Tornadoes are like Jesus. They show up when you're not expecting them. Anyone who has spent any time living in tornado alley knows exactly what I'm talking about.

You West Texas ladies know what I'm talkin' about, don't you? Y'know, you're driving your kids to school in your Escalade and as you're tooling along putting on eyeliner with one hand, texting with the other, typing on your laptop with your left foot, and writing a note with your mouth, you glance up and notice clouds building up in the west-north-west, which means that you might get some rain later on in the afternoon.

No biggie.

The storm looks several hours away.

No cause for alarm.

So, as usual, you drop your rugrats off at prison, I mean public school, and customarily, after your morning errands, you head off to Starbucks for your ritual half-decaf, skinny, Frappuccino with spiced, spider monkey milk, and to meet your lover, sorry, your *prayer partner*, named Todd, who is sassy hipster, lactose intolerant, and sports a pinky ring.

As you're walking across the parking lot, dreaming about what you and Todd will do today and where you will do it, things get eerily still. Just before you open the door to Starbucks, you feel the barometric pressure drop, which causes you to look up. Low and behold, that distant thunderhead is now right on top of you and is a black wall of voodoo that's got the finger of God, a death-dealing, F-4 twister coming out of the wall cloud. Immediately you grab the door to try to get in and find some structure to hide behind, but you're too late. The tornado sucks you into a natural disaster, you're transported to Oz, surrounded by flying devil monkeys, and you're now conversing with a cowardly tin man.

That's why I hate tornados.

I have enough unexpected bunkum going on without having the violent vortex variable added to *mi vida*.

Hurricanes, though wickedly devastating, give you about a month to get the *hizzle* out of the way. If you die in a hurricane, you're stupid. Or you're deaf, blind, and don't have any friends. The NOAA dudes over-warn us during the hurricane's approach, for God's sake. They don't just show up like a tornado. They waddle across the Atlantic like a drunk bumping across a nightclub dance floor after seven *Cuervo* shots. The weather boys now are pretty spot on as to where the 'cane is going to make landfall. Tornados on the other hand drop out of the sky like Jason Voorhees, flinging cows, wielding a machete, and making you run through sheet rock.

According to Jesus' first sermon, when He shot across the bow of us booger-picking mortals, He promised both the good and bad, those who "built well," and those who built a rat trap, the holy and the profane, Mother Teresa and Sista Souljah, one and all, will get slammed-danced in this life.

That's both crews. The goodies and the baddies.

Not just the evil weeds.

All of us.

He formally forewarned everybody sucking air to brace for life's crunch. Rains ...Floods ... Winds ... will burst against our "house."

I wonder what "burst" means in the Greek?

I'm guessin' it solidly falls into the "bad crap" category.

Dear Christian: Your Fear is Full of Crap

No doubt, some of you are thinking, "Why *would* a good God allow bad things to happen to good people?" Good people? I don't know who these good people are. I keep bumping into sinners everywhere I go.

C'mon, folks. Can't we drop the "I'm a good person stuff," like right now? Because according to the Bible, we're all turds, or more properly put, lost, wrapped in sin, and covered with rebellious sauce. And if we got what we deserved we would not be happy, Clappy.

> *There's nobody living right, not even one, nobody who knows the score, nobody alert for God. They've all taken the wrong turn; they've all wandered down blind alleys. No one's living right; I can't find a single one. Their throats are open graves, their tongues slick as mud slides. Every word they speak is tinged with poison. They open their with heartbreak and ruin, don't know the first thing about living with others. They never give God the time of day ... we've compiled this long and sorry record as sinners (both us and them) and proved that we are utterly incapable of living the glorious lives God wills for us ...(Rom. 3:10-18; 23, MSG)*

Here's an acid test for those still not convinced that they're "all that bad" and thus don't "deserve" a storm. Allow my buddy, Slappy White, to wiretap your phone, record all private conversations and text messages, and video all your actions for the next year. Then, after the year of twenty-four/seven surveillance, Slappy will take all of your less-than-shiny moments and put them on YouTube for the whole globe to take a gander. I'm not a gambling man, but if I were, after that video goes online, I'd be willing to wager that you wouldn't be talking the "I'm a good person" smack any longer.

Why is pain a part of the human experience? Why God allows what He does, I don't pretend to know. Heck, I can't even figure out women or smart phones; how am I supposed to know what's going on in His divine noggin'?

If you've got the time to wade into such weighty topics, go ahead; knock yourself out. I will gladly let all you heavy-thinking wizards wrap your brain around its axle with philosophical inquiries into the quandary of human suffering in relation to God's omnipotence and His benevolence. Go for it.

So, little ol' redneck me will simply take the Son of God's word for it that storms are coming. We're all gonna go through hell, so I'm trying to prep for it as well as a goofy, Spirit-led sinner can when it comes knocking on my door because Jesus told us it is not a matter of *if* storms will come, but *when* storms will come.

To be forewarned is forearmed, eh?

So, let's just dispense with the, "I'm good and I don't deserve storms," blather. If we got what we deserved for what we have said and done, to both God and men, we'd be in the crunchy bucket at KFC. I personally cannot believe that I haven't gone, and don't continue to go, through major tsunamis every day for my past, present, and future sinfulness. The only thing I merit is a front row seat on the eighth concentric circle of Dante's *Inferno*. Yes, I wonder why a good God would allow *good* things to happen to a bad Doug.

What we do know about why God allows storms to come is gathered in the pronouncement of their pending presence -- they are foundation testers. Storms, plain and simple, are provers of the substance of our subsistence.

They're just a test.

Like all tests, if we have done our due diligence, we'll be okay.

I remember when I went to work for Sam's Club back in college. If we made it through the initial interviewing process, we had to undergo one last screening, namely, the pee in the Dixie cup drug test. Since I hadn't been doing blow or bong

Dear Christian: Your Fear is Full of Crap

hits for quite some time, I sailed through with flying colors. My dope smokin' buddy we nicknamed Awood, was not so lucky on his urination examination. His pee was loaded down with more THC than Snoop Dogg's entire fleet of bongs. Poor Awood.

I view storms as life's midterms, presented to make us fit for our final exam. Of course, this final assessment is a little graver than it would be, say, for one's English Lit course. If we fail Heaven's final, we will not *get* an F. We will *be* F'd -- meaning forsaken, of course. And we cannot retake the course.

Yep, storms tell on us.

They reveal how we have built our lives.

If we have built our existence on His Word, He said we'd ride the storm out. However, if we have been bull-headed and have built it on our own BS (belief systems) or have taken our cue from cultural crud, the storms will be a reality blast to a life ill founded.

Let me ask you a question.

Would you think I was a moron if I bought a double wide trailer house, put its skids on a stack of cinderblocks right on a South Florida beach, and then expected that barely anchored, flimsy structure to survive a Cat 5 hurricane?

Short answer – duh.

In addition, would I sound goofy if, after a wicked storm obliterated my feeble, beach-based bungalow and I was wedged thirty feet up in a palm tree with a coconut stuck up my backside, I told the weather chick from *Channel 7 News* who was reporting on the aftermath of the storm that I didn't know why God would allow this to happen to me?

Why would God allow this to happen to me, indeed?

Hey, someone get a stupid sticker and put it on my forehead. Get a pellet gun and shoot me.

Why did *God?!*

I'll tell me why. I'm an idiot. I built a hurricane magnet in hurricane central. I blew off wisdom, building codes, common sense, and erected a house of cards in a hurricane corridor. Had I built to post-hurricane Andrew stringent standards, there would have been a fair–to-middlin' chance that my house would have made it through a brutal storm with only a few downed trees and assorted debris.

But no. I built crap, and crap happened.

Pause and meditate.

In summation, little kiddies, what is the first impression Jesus put to us critters in Matthew's account of His initial major address? Expect storms. I said, He said, we should ... expect storms. We should live in light of having, at times, the snot kicked out of us spiritually, physically, nationally, financially, emotionally, relationally, etc.

What else did He brand us with?

Build well.

Don't put a trailer house on the beach and expect it to endure 150 mph winds and a twenty-foot storm surge. In lieu of all of us being in line for some sort of storm, Jesus exhorts us to build well, and even though He won't exempt us from garbage, He told us we will survive, even thrive, when the poop hits the fan -- if, *if,* we build our lives on the principles of His Word.

Storms are coming.

That was one of the first things out of His mouth during His earthly ministry.

That's what He impressed upon His disciples. His message hasn't changed.

Are we ready?

Culture Warrior Battle Notes

Chapter Sixteen: The Warriors' Confession

"Prayer is not an argument with God to persuade Him to move things our way, but an exercise by which we are enabled by His Spirit to move ourselves His way."
– Leonard Ravenhill

I know. The title of this chapter sounds a bit like a tawdry Harlequin novel that the *Desperate Housewives of Orange County* would be into, right?

Either that or, some Special Operator's version of *50 Shades of Gray.*

Never fear. Doug is here and it has *nada* to do with that mess.

What you do have in your hands, my fellow combatant, is spiritual dynamite to demonic strongholds that seek to derail God's eternal purpose for this planet which includes you fulfilling his high calling for your life.

What's that you say?

You didn't know you were in a raging spiritual battle that has been blowing and going since the dawn of man?

Well, let me help you here.

Dear Christian: if you're a believer, then you're in a spiritual war whether you like it or not. *Ergo*, you are a warrior and you're either a good, bad, or ugly one.

The upshot is, if you suck at spiritual warfare, there's hope. God can train your "hands for war" (Ps. 18:34). He wants you to excel more than you and your mommy do.

For you to excel in spiritual warfare means His Son is exalted, the devil gets a mega scar in his defeated backside, souls are freed from demonic darkness, and the culture gets leavened with righteousness, peace, and joy in the Holy Ghost.

Yep, Christian, there's holy greatness wrapped up in you being an adept wielder of the weapons of our warfare. So, don't take kicking demonic butt lightly, my friend. Souls and society are at stake.

This chapter's goal is simple: my sole focus is to supply you with the biblical fodder to believe and speak when God calls you to open up a 64-ounce-can-of-whup-ass when Satan tries to thwart God's kingdom expansion.

Now, when I'm talking about confessions, I'm not talking about just confessing you're a goofball in general or that you're addicted to watching *Keeping Up With The Kardashians* re-runs.

That's a whole different topic for an entirely different book.

The confession that I'm concerned about is that which tumbles out of your mouth and whether or not it lines up with what God has declared once you run into troubles in the midst of battle.

What we think and say, when we're in the midst of a storm, is *muy importante*. If you think I'm full of crap read Numbers 13.

Succinctly, if you think you're done -- you're done.

If you think you're gonna pull out of whatever garbage

you're currently mired in there's a 99.9% chance that soon you'll be footloose and fancy free from life's quicksand. Or as Jesus put it in Mt.17:20 …

> *"The simple truth is that if you had a mere kernel of faith, a poppy seed, say, you would tell this mountain, 'Move!' and it would move. There is nothing you wouldn't be able to tackle." (MSG)*

Please note that Jesus said for your mountain to move you have to speak to it. Which means you gotta get rowdy with your yapper. Talk biblical, Holy Ghost, trash to your mountains, obstacles and whatever devils are attempting to best you.

Get loud declaring God's word over your sad situation.

Everything smells, so attitude sells.

Confess God's promises over your life with passion, faith, authority, and yes, once again, attitude.

The tongue is powerful.

According to James an unbridled tongue can unleash hell in your life. Check it out …

> *Even so the tongue is a little member, and boasteth great things. Behold, how great a matter a little fire kindleth! And the tongue is a fire, a world of iniquity: so is the tongue among our members, that it defileth the whole body, and setteth on fire the course of nature; and it is set on fire of hell. James 3:5-6 (KJV)*

And according to Jesus, you can overcome Satan by Christ's shed blood, not being afraid of death and … via the word of your testimony. Yes, Christian, what you say has massive weight tied to it for good or for evil in your life. Behold, I give you example number 13,998,807,004.

> *7 And there was war in heaven: Michael and his angels fought against the dragon; and the dragon fought and his angels,*
>
> *8 And prevailed not; neither was their place found any more in heaven.*
>
> *9 And the great dragon was cast out, that old serpent, called the Devil, and Satan, which deceiveth the whole world: he was cast out into the earth, and his angels were cast out with him.*
>
> *10 And I heard a loud voice saying in heaven, Now is come salvation, and strength, and the kingdom of our God, and the power of his Christ: for the accuser of our brethren is cast down, which accused them before our God day and night.*
>
> *11 And they overcame him by the blood of the Lamb, and by the word of their testimony; and they loved not their lives unto the death.*
>
> *12 Therefore rejoice, ye heavens, and ye that dwell in them. Woe to the inhabiters of the earth and of the sea! for the devil is come down unto you, having great wrath, because he knoweth that he hath but a short time. Rev. 12:7-12 (NASB)*

When Satan tempted Jesus in the wilderness, he did it with his words.

He didn't show Jesus some porn sketches he'd drawn.

He didn't do it with a Rolex that he dangled in front of an impoverished Christ.

He used his words to tempt Jesus with the lust of the flesh, lust of the eyes, and the boastful pride of life.

So … how did Jesus react when He was getting the best Beelzebub could toss at Him?

Dear Christian: Your Fear is Full of Crap

Well, let's check it out …

1 Then was Jesus led up of the Spirit into the wilderness to be tempted of the devil.

2 And when he had fasted forty days and forty nights, he was afterward an hungred.

3 And when the tempter came to him, he said, If thou be the Son of God, command that these stones be made bread.

4 But he answered and said, It is written, Man shall not live by bread alone, but by every word that proceedeth out of the mouth of God.

5 Then the devil taketh him up into the holy city, and setteth him on a pinnacle of the temple,

6 And saith unto him, If thou be the Son of God, cast thyself down: for it is written, He shall give his angels charge concerning thee: and in their hands they shall bear thee up, lest at any time thou dash thy foot against a stone.

7 Jesus said unto him, It is written again, Thou shalt not tempt the Lord thy God.

8 Again, the devil taketh him up into an exceeding high mountain, and sheweth him all the kingdoms of the world, and the glory of them;

9 And saith unto him, All these things will I give thee, if thou wilt fall down and worship me.

10 Then saith Jesus unto him, Get thee hence, Satan: for it is written, Thou shalt worship the Lord thy God, and him only shalt thou serve.

11 Then the devil leaveth him, and, behold, angels came and ministered unto him. Matt. 4:1-11 (NASB)

Jesus countered *el Diablo*'s lies with the word of God.

Please note ...

1. Jesus didn't quote Oprah.

2. Jesus didn't quote the virgin Mary.

3. Jesus didn't quote a positive meme He saw on Instagram.

4. Jesus didn't quote Tony Robbins.

5. Jesus didn't quote the lyrics from Katy Perry's song, *Roar!*

6. Jesus didn't quote The Pope.

7. Jesus didn't quote The Southern Baptist Convention.

He quoted the word of God.

Jesus fought Satan's words, which included a scripture Satan had twisted, with the *verbum Dei,* and it worked. Shocker, eh?

Jesus spanked Lucifer with epic scriptural counterpunches and the Slithering One left black-eyed with his tail between his legs.

Indeed, Jesus talked back to the Devil, with the word of God, and so should you.

The word of God has power, folks. Hello. Peter put it this way ...

> *Grace and peace be multiplied unto you through the knowledge of God, and of Jesus our Lord, According as his divine power hath given unto us all things that pertain unto life and godliness, through the knowledge of him that hath called us to glory and virtue: Whereby are given unto us exceeding great and precious promises: that by these ye might be partakers of the divine nature, having escaped the corruption that is in the world through lust. 2Pet. 1: 2-4 (NASB)*

The writer of Hebrews says the word is sharper than

sword.

> *For the word of God is quick, and powerful, and sharper than any two-edged sword, piercing even to the dividing asunder of soul and spirit, and of the joints and marrow, and is a discerner of the thoughts and intents of the heart. Heb. 4:12 (NASB)*

That's why Satan wants you to be an idiot swordsman, ignorant of the word of God, because Christ's word in your mouth mixed with a summit or plummet faith is a flippin' nightmare for the Nefarious One.

Look what the apostle Paul said about the word of God coming out of your mouth …

So what exactly was Moses saying?

The word that saves is right here,

> as near as the tongue in your mouth,

> as close as the heart in your chest.

> *8 But what saith it? The word is nigh thee, even in thy mouth, and in thy heart: that is, the word of faith, which we preach;*

> *9 That if thou shalt confess with thy mouth the Lord Jesus, and shalt believe in thine heart that God hath raised him from the dead, thou shalt be saved.*

> *10 For with the heart man believeth unto righteousness; and with the mouth confession is made unto salvation. Rom. 10:8-10 (NASB)*

Incredible. Believe and speak and boom … God goes to work in your life. Not only in saving our sin-cursed souls but in regard to all things that pertain to life and godliness.

So, yeah … your words matter.

Doug Giles

While everyone else is yapping about fear, doubt, death, and disaster you should declare from God's word fearlessness, faith, life, and His Kingdom come. Can you dig it? I knew you could.

Speak God's word over your current dilemma and watch Him go to work kicking butt and taking names for His glory and on your behalf.

Agree with God's promises instead of the fear "The News" trades in.

Herewith are some glorious promises, in just a few categories, that you should start shouting from the rooftops, ASAP.

If you're sweating finances declare this …

31 Therefore take no thought, saying, What shall we eat? or, What shall we drink? or, Wherewithal shall we be clothed?

32 (For after all these things do the Gentiles seek:) for your heavenly Father knoweth that ye have need of all these things.

33 But seek ye first the kingdom of God, and his righteousness; and all these things shall be added unto you.

34 Take therefore no thought for the morrow: for the morrow shall take thought for the things of itself. Sufficient unto the day is the evil thereof. Matt. 6:31-34 (NASB)

And God is able to make all grace abound toward you; that ye, always having all sufficiency in all things, may abound to every good work: (As it is written, He hath dispersed abroad; he hath given to the poor: his righteousness remaineth for ever. Now he that ministereth seed to the sower both minister bread for your food, and multiply your seed sown, and increase the fruits of your righteousness;) Being enriched in every thing to

Dear Christian: Your Fear is Full of Crap

all bountifulness, which causeth through us thanksgiving to God. 2Cor. 9: 8-11 (NASB)

If you've been caught up in the "The Media's" mass delusional psychosis and you're worried about health, your job, our nation and your kid's future; shout these bad boys at the devil and his defeated ilk...

"For God hath not given us the spirit of fear; but of power, and of love, and of a sound mind." 2Tim. 1:7 (NASB)

"No weapon that is formed against thee shall prosper; and every tongue that shall rise against thee in judgment thou shalt condemn. This is the heritage of the servants of the Lord, and their righteousness is of me, saith the Lord." Isa. 54:17 (NASB)

"What time I am afraid, I will trust in thee. In God I will praise his word, in God I have put my trust; I will not fear what flesh can do unto me." Ps. 56:3-4 (NASB)

"I will not be afraid of ten thousands of people, that have set themselves against me round about. Arise, O Lord; save me, O my God: for thou hast smitten all mine enemies upon the cheek bone; thou hast broken the teeth of the ungodly. Salvation belongeth unto the Lord: thy blessing is upon thy people." Ps. 3.6-8 (NASB)

"Those who live in the shelter of the Most High will find rest in the shadow of the Almighty. This I declare about the Lord: He alone is my refuge, my place of safety; he is my God, and I trust him. For he will rescue you from every trap and protect you from deadly disease." Ps. 91:1-3 (NASB) [Read this entire chapter.]

"Don't worry about anything; instead, pray about everything. Tell God what you need, and thank him for all he has done." Phil. 4:6 (NASB)

7 having cast all your anxiety on Him, because He

cares about you. 1Pet. 5:7 (NASB)

33 These things I have spoken to you so that in Me you may have peace. In the world you have tribulation, but take courage; I have overcome the world." John 16:33 (NASB)

7 The Lord is good, A stronghold in the day of trouble, And He knows those who take refuge in Him. Nah. 1:7 (NASB)

"Don't worry about anything; instead, pray about everything. Tell God what you need, and thank him for all he has done." Phil. 4:6 (NLT)

"What shall we say about such wonderful things as these? If God is for us, who can ever be against us?" Rom. 8:31 (NLT)

"The faithful love of the Lord never ends! His mercies never cease. Great is his faithfulness; his mercies begin afresh each morning." Lam. 3:22-23 (NLT)

"We are God's masterpiece. He has created us anew in Christ Jesus, so we can do the good things he planned for us long ago." Eph. 2:10 (NLT)

Boldly confessing and obeying His word is how we "resist the Devil" causing him to flee from us and our land (1Pet. 5:8,9)

Paul put it this way …

"For the report of your obedience has reached everyone; therefore I am rejoicing over you, but I want you to be wise in what is good, and innocent in what is evil. The God of peace will soon crush Satan under your feet. The grace of our Lord Jesus be with you." Rom. 16: 19-20 (NASB)

Culture Warrior Battle Notes

Chapter Seventeen: Pastors Who Defied The Ubiquitous COVIDictators

"Ministers who do not spend two hours a day in prayer are not worth a dime a dozen, degrees or no degrees."
– Leonard Ravenhill

My news portal, ClashDaily.com (270M page views), has been covering from the get-go the disgusting way civil magistrates and their jackbooted thugs have harassed pastors and their congregants who wouldn't lockdown and/or didn't buy Mayor McCheese's bogus mask and social distancing mandates. Which we all know now were complete and utter, can't scrape it off your shoe, crap. Yes, their edicts did nothing to cudgel off the giving or the receiving of the bad cold from Wuhan. To my knowledge, none of these elected dipsticks in the U.S. or Canada or elsewhere have apologized for the atrocious way Christians and Pastors were treated.

Below are a scant few posts out of many written by my epic editors and friends over at ClashDaily.com, Wes and Karen Walker. These posts spotlight both the abuses of the out of control, control freaks and a few pastors who wouldn't put up with the overlord's bullcrap.

You can find a lot more articles and videos of how horrible Churches were treated from 2020-2021+ via ClashDaily.com. Once over at our site search for "Covid … Church … Pastor".

Florida Pastor Says Church And Bible School Will Remain Open 'We're Raising Up Revivalists, Not Pansies'

Written by: K. Walker on March 18, 2020

Is this an exercise in faith, or a really dumb idea? We report, you decide.

Pastor Rodney Howard Browne, an evangelical minister who runs a church and Bible school in Tampa, Florida is committed to keeping the church doors open no matter what.

Services are going on as usual, as is teaching in the Bible school.

He's even encouraging churchgoers to greet each other with handshakes.

'We are not stopping anything, Pastor Rodney Howard-Browne told his followers during a sermon at River Tampa Church on Monday.

'I've got news for you, this church will never close.

'The only time the church will close is when the Rapture is taking place.

Dear Christian: Your Fear is Full of Crap

'This Bible school is open because we're raising up revivalists, not pansies.'

Some jurisdictions have issued bans on gatherings of 250 people or more.

Florida has seen a spike in the number of people who have tested positive for the Wuhan Virus, climbing up to 155 on Monday, and four confirmed deaths.

Still, many think that the precautions are excessive and are actually causing panic, not to mention the financial damage to families in lower-income brackets, workers in the service industry, and those living paycheck to paycheck.

Browne says that the church is the safest place to be in a crisis.

Of course, the media have to take shots at the minister who has a different worldview than they do.

'Listen, this has to be the safest place,' he said during the sermon.

'If you cannot be saved in church, you are in serious trouble.'

Last month, Howard-Browne bragged that he had plans to stop the coronavirus.

He said he would do to the pathogen what he did with the Zika virus, which was 'cursed' from Florida in the name of Jesus.

*Source: Daily Mail_*

Doug Giles

Thousands Sign Petition To Have Pastor ARRESTED For Violating State Ban On Large Gatherings

Written by: K. Walker on March 25, 2020

Is the Pastor wrong to continue to hold church services in defiance of the state ban, or is this a "religious freedom" issue?

In an online petition calling for his arrest, a Baton Rouge pastor has been accused of endangering lives for continuing to hold church services after Louisiana Governor John Bel Edwards imposed on March 16 banning gatherings larger than 50 people to prevent the spread of COVID-19.

Reverend Tony Spell, leader of the Life Tabernacle Church in Baton Rouge, led 1,825 congregants in worship on Sunday and said there would be a further service on Tuesday evening.

Police had warned Pastor Spell that the National Guard would be sent in to disperse parishioners if he continued to hold his gatherings.

The *Daily Mail* article includes that Louisiana has had the "fastest growth rate" in the number of cases but that's because testing for COVID-19 has ramped up in just the last few days and the results are now flooding in.

This despite Gov. John Bel Edwards' order against gatherings of more than 50 people as the number infected in the state rose to more than 1,300 yesterday, including 46 deaths.

Indeed, Louisiana has the fastest growth rate for cases in the world and Gov. Edwards warned just days ago the state could 'be the next Italy.'

Source: Daily Mail

Also, as the *Los Angeles Times* notes, Mari Gras is likely how the coronavirus spread in Baton Rouge in the first place.

The stakes are particularly high in Louisiana, where doctors say large gatherings during Mardi Gras last month likely fostered COVID-19, now spreading faster there than anywhere else in the world, with 1,388 cases and 46 deaths, most of those in New Orleans.

"Most infections in this area occurred during Mardi Gras. There was probably a tremendous number of people infected then, probably with no symptoms," said Dr. Brobson Lutz, former director of New Orleans Health Department.

Source: L.A. Times

But hey, let's pick on the church, right?

The Change.org petition includes the following:

On Sunday, March 22, despite personal pleas to not defy the order again by opening his church by current Louisiana Governor John Bel Edwards, Tony Spell continued to defy orders that are in place to save his fellow citizens. 1800 people attended his immoral and unauthorized money plate collection meeting, what his flock calls "Sunday church."

(That seems a wee bit prejudiced, no?)

We the people of this same area, already hard hit by more than our share of Coronavirus Covid-19 infections, believe that this charlatan and his brother cousin Tim are premeditated killers who must be stopped and held responsible for their sick and selfish actions. We ask our Governor to have Spell arrested immediately and charged with 1800 counts of reckless endangerment for a start, for the countless lives he will be brutalizing and even ending with his selfishness and ignorance. We further ask that he be made personally to answer legally for each and every infection and death in the 5 parishes surrounding his church in East Baton Rouge Parish occurring anytime after 17 March 2020.

Cool story, bro. Now do the local mosque.

If they arrest Pastor Spell, that's up to local law enforcement, but whoever wrote this petition is defaming the man by calling him a "premeditated killer" who is "brutalizing" lives. Maybe the author should face a lawsuit for that.

There are all sorts of information in the *Daily Mail* article that has painted Pastor Spell as a nutter who claims that the virus is political. He's not denying that the virus is real, or a threat, nor is he compelling people to attend. He does, like many other Christians, hold to the belief that God indeed heals people.

Dear Christian: Your Fear is Full of Crap

Florida Pastor Arrested And Charged For Disregarding State Mandate Forbidding Church Attendance

Written by: Wes Walker on March 30, 2020

Nearly 20 centuries before journalists and university profs were 'speaking truth to power' Christians were doing so at the cost of their very lives. Should this news really surprise us?

With the rise of this viral outbreak, the government has ordered religious groups NOT to assemble and worship as per their custom.

It should surprise exactly ZERO people familiar either with American history or the history of Christian believers that some American believers have looked back at their government and said — calmly but firmly — that simply isn't the government's decision to make.

Christians through history have met in dangerous settings. Recently it has been secret meetings in communist China and Soviet bloc nations — knowing that arrest would lead to the worst kinds of prisons. Or Christians meeting to pray neck-deep in the swamp overnight during Idi Amin's evil dictatorship in Uganda. Or in many Muslim countries where 'blasphemy' or conversion are illegal still today.

Christians in the past have often welcomed death rather than obey sacrilegious imperatives given by pagan or apostate governments. The first-century church exploded in growth when Romans watched as *we* were the ones caring for plague victims.

In the third century AD, an epidemic swept across Northern Africa, Italy, and the western empire. As many as 5000 people a day were dying in Rome. The sick were abandoned in the streets and the dead left unburied. In Carthage, the Christians were blamed for the disease, and the emperor ordered Christians to sacrifice to their gods to end it. Carthage's bishop, Cyprian, encouraged Christians to care for the sick and dying. They buried the dead and risked getting sick by taking in the sick. This was repeated other times in the early centuries of the church during epidemics. Christians introduced a new concern and standard of care for sick people. — STR

Now, faced with an illness that can seemingly barely hold a candle to Ebola, let alone the Black Death, non-essential people were sent home, while those essential to society — like grocery stores, pharmacies, and take-out food — remain open.

Pastor Howard-Browne defended that decision in a Facebook live post titled "End of Days Part Three."

"I'm not again negating that people are dying from the coronavirus," he said. "We're not saying that, just saying that the thing is blown totally way out of proportion and if you shut the church down, the church is not a non-essential service." —_Fox

A Florida pastor just isn't buying the idea that pastoral care and Christian worship are non-essential.

Dear Christian: Your Fear is Full of Crap

Local governments around the country are urging Americans to stay at home and avoid large social gatherings to limit the spread of COVID-19. Despite those orders, several large churches around the country opened their doors to hundreds of people.

In Florida, The River at Tampa Bay Church remained open Sunday to the public despite a "Safer At Home" order issued by the county — an order that includes places of worship. While the church is encouraged sick parishioners to stay home and view services online, the church said in a statement that it felt obligated to stay open.

"We expect our police and firefighters to be ready and available to rescue and to help and to keep the peace," the church said in a statement. "The Church is another one of those essential services. It is a place where people turn for help and for comfort in a climate of fear and uncertainty. Therefore, we feel that it would be wrong for us to close our doors on them, at this time, or any time."

On Monday, Hillsborough County Sheriff's Office arrested the church's pastor, Rodney Howard-Browne. He's charged with unlawful assembly and violation of a public health emergency order.

"His reckless disregard for human life put hundreds of people in his congregation at risk, and thousands of residents who may interact with them this week in danger," Hillsborough County Sheriff Chad Chronister said.

The River wasn't the only large church to hold services on Sunday. In Turtlecreek Township, Ohio — just north of Cincinnati — Solid Rock Church has held in-person services the last two Sundays, despite a "Stay At Home" order from Ohio Gov. Mike DeWine. — Source: WXYZ

Doug Giles

Putting The 'Protest' In Protestant -- Cali Megachurch FULLY Reopens And Files Lawsuit Against Gov. Newsom

Written by: K. Walker on August 14, 2020

Pastor John MacArthur of Grace Community Church has decided to follow God and not Caesar when it comes to holding in-person worship services.

Grace Community Church in suburban Los Angeles is now holding large in-person worship services in open defiance of the limit placed by the California government.

The Newsom administration in California placed a limit on in-person worship services to a gathering of 25% building capacity to a maximum of 100 people.

The services at GCC are being held with 7,000 in attendance.

A megachurch in suburban Los Angeles which has defied public health orders to hold services with up to 7,000 worshipers has filed a lawsuit challenging California's 100-person limit on indoor church gatherings.

Grace Community Church in Sun Valley initially closed its doors in March with the arrival of the COVID-19 pandemic, but in recent weeks it has flouted public health guidelines and allowed thousands into its congregation.

It initially had plans to formally reopen in May, but a federal court ruling upheld the state's ban on indoor

Dear Christian: Your Fear is Full of Crap

religious services. Grace Community Church re-opened in July.

You can't really blame MacArthur for flouting the laws -- between May and July the world changed.

Suddenly, we learned that there were things that were worth the risk of contracting a virus that (according to Worldometer) more than 99% of people who contract it recover from -- protesting the death of a black man who had a police officer kneeling on his neck for nearly 9 minutes; protesting police brutality in general; tearing down statues of anyone who might suggest that America *isn't* an awful country; and outright rioting. We had "medical experts" excusing the behavior because the virus would somehow be prevented by opposing *"systemic racism."* Oh, and attending protests with hundreds or even *thousands* of people wasn't something that the "contact tracers" were going to ask about.

What wasn't on the list of acceptable risks was attending a worship service.

Doug Giles

Canadian Pastor Incarcerated For Prioritizing Divine Authority Above Government

Written by: Wes Walker on February 19, 2021

There comes a time in everyone's life where you have to draw a line in the sand and decide whether you live by your convictions or fold like a cheap suit. This man stood.

Two competing forces were pulling Rev. James Coates of GraceLife Church of Edmonton in opposite directions. Government institutions demanded his compliance in shutting down religious gatherings. The divine approval of a historical precedent of the Apostles preaching contrary to such orders, as we saw all through the book of Acts pulled him the other direction.

Ultimately, Coates has chosen to offend man by obeying God, rather than reversing that dynamic.

He turned himself in to police on Tuesday after defying a court order to stop holding services.

His lawyer, James Kitchen with the Justice Centre for Constitutional Freedoms, said Coates was still in the queue as of 2 p.m.

"His first obedience is to his Lord, is to his God. And normally, obeying Jesus and obeying the government go right in hand," Kitchen told CTV News Edmonton that afternoon. "The government's forcing him in to a position where he has to choose between disobeying God and obeying government, or obeying God and disobeying government."

Dear Christian: Your Fear is Full of Crap

The church was first cited for, among other things, hosting more than 15 per cent of its capacity at a December service. Coates was fined $1,200. A Court of Queen's Bench order to enforce Alberta's public health order was issued in January when it continued to break gathering, masking, and physical distancing rules.

GraceLife has met for three consecutive weeks after it was ordered to close at the end of January. The second time, Coates was arrested and served the undertaking.

"Ultimately what Coates and GraceLife is doing is exercising their constitutionally protected rights under Section 2 of the Charter," Kitchen said.

"The CMOH orders infringe those freedoms and the enforcement of the CMOH orders infringes those freedoms."

According to the lawyer, Coates – who has refused to address media except in statements posted online or at the beginning of Sunday services – and the GraceLife community reject COVID-19 restrictions as "an evil that has to stop." -- CTV

Here is where this story gets interesting. He remains locked up because he is standing on those same principles. He is unwilling to accept the bail conditions they have offered, not because he is superficially 'defiant', but because he rejects the premise that his first allegiance is to the state and his personal well-being ahead of the commandment of God.

There was a bail hearing on Wednesday morning and Coates "was to be released on conditions." However, "he continued to refuse to agree with those conditions and a judge's order was issued compelling him to attend court on Wednesday, Feb. 24," RCMP said in a news release.

"We've been consistent in our approach of escalated levels of enforcement with Pastor Coates, and we were hopeful to resolve this issue in a different manner," Lokken said.

"The pastor's actions, and the subsequent effects those actions could have on the health and safety of citizens dictated our response in this situation." – Global News

This news story, both by the stand this one man is taking, and the government ultimatum prompts an uncomfortable question:

How many Christians, religious leaders included, wouldn't be in even the slightest danger if preaching the gospel were legally forbidden?

Dear Christian: Your Fear is Full of Crap

COVID GESTAPO: Pastor Pawlowski Returns To Canada ... And Is Immediately Arrested

Written by: Wes Walker on September 28, 2021

You may remember the Canadian Pastor who chased the police out of his Church when they tried to interrupt a church service during Holy Week. He's back in the news.

Artur Pawlowski went viral when he called the police enforcement the 'Gestapo' for descending on a Church service. This was not the first brush he had with the law... his city had previously been giving him legal grief over giving free food to the homeless.

From an earlier article we ran about his story...

In 2005, Pawlowski was receiving fines for preaching outside of Calgary City Hall and feeding the homeless through the charity he founded. His alleged offenses included reading the Bible aloud, using a megaphone, and stretching an extension cord across a city sidewalk.

Police eventually waited until he had left a Sunday service, followed him onto the highway, and arrested him right there on the road. We covered some of the developments of that story.

Not surprisingly, his story quickly attracted attention in the US, where that story generated enough interest that he was invited to speak publicly at a number of venues, including one in Portland that attracted the attention of Antifa agitators.

When he returned to the city of Calgary, he was met by police while he was still on the tarmac.

At the time Pastor Pawlowski was taken into custody, no word was given to his waiting family members about why he was being arrested, the nature of his charges, or even where he was being taken.

Here's a question for you: did your pastor or priest obey civil magistrates, or did they defy them like the aforementioned men of God did?

Culture Warrior Battle Notes

Chapter Eighteen: Here Are 49 More Things To Shout At The Devil

"The man who can get believers to praying would, under God, usher in the greatest revival that the world has ever known."
– Leonard Ravenhill

Pastors nowadays refer to Jesus as one's "personal Savior".

How quaint, eh?

In Psalm 59, David, being the constantly in trouble child of God that he was, saw God not just as some amorphous "personal Savior" but referred to God as ...

1. Lord God of Hosts ("Hosts" means, "Angelic armies").

2. The God of my mercy.

3. O Lord our Shield.

4. The God who rules to the ends of the earth.

5. God of my defense.

Matter of fact, David had a litany of names and descriptions for the Shepherd of his soul throughout the Psalms. Shout these out God at the top of your lungs when the enemy is attacking you, the Church, our families, and our great nation. God's a holy butt-kicker against all that is evil and the clowns who're attached to Satan's devices.

Check 'em out ...

Names of God in the Book of Psalms

The Lord – 1:2

God of my righteousness – 4:1 My King – 5:2

Oh Lord my God – 7:1

God of my salvation – 18:46

God of Jacob – 20:1

Oh My Strength – 22:19

King of Glory – 29:3

Oh Lord God of Truth – 31:5

The Lord God of Israel – 41:13

Oh Mighty One – 45:3

The King of all the earth – 47:7

God of Abraham – 47:9

God of the Most High – 57:2

YAH – 68:4

The Almighty – 68:14

God the Lord – 68:20

Oh Holy One of Israel – 71:22

Oh Shepherd of Israel – 80:1

The Lord our Maker – 95:6

God their Savior – 106:21

The Mighty One of Jacob – 132:2

The God of Gods – 136:2

The God of heaven – 136:26

Descriptions of God in the Book of Psalms

A shield for me – 3:3

My glory – 3:3

The One who lifts up my head – 3:3

The righteous God – 7:9

A just judge – 7:11

A refuge – 9:9

The portion of my inheritance and my cup – 16:5

My strength – 18:1

The Lord is my rock and my fortress and my deliverer – 18:2

The horn of my salvation, stronghold – 18:2

My support – 18:18

My shepherd – 23:1

My light and my salvation – 27:1

The strength of my life – 27:1

The saving refuge of His anointed – 28:8

My helper – 30:10

Rock of refuge – 31:2

My hiding place – 32:7

My help and my deliverer – 41:17

The God of my life – 42:8

My exceeding joy – 43:4

A very present help in trouble 46:1

Our guide even to death – 48:14

My defense – 59:9

My God of mercy – 59:10

A shelter of me, a strong tower from the enemy – 61:3

A father of the fatherless, a defender of widows – 68:5

The strength of my heart and my portion forever – 73:26

The great God and the great King above all gods – 95:3

He who keeps Israel – 121:4

Your shade at your right hand – 121:5

My portion in the land of the living – 142:5

My high tower – 144:2

Work those titles and descriptions of God into your fervent prayers and into your worship and watch what God does to the powers of darkness when they try to assail you.

Dear Christian: Your Fear is Full of Crap

Culture Warrior Battle Notes

Chapter Nineteen: Five Imprecatory Psalms Against Wicked Leaders

"The true man of God is heartsick, grieved at the worldliness of the Church, grieved at the toleration of sin in the Church, grieved at the prayerlessness in the Church. He is disturbed that the corporate prayer of the Church no longer pulls down the strongholds of the devil."
– Leonard Ravenhill

The following is from my #1 Amazon bestselling book (for 25 straight weeks) titled, *Psalms of War: Prayers That Literally Kick Ass.* Try praying these prayers out loud next time you and your Christian buddies get together. They're epic. However, they could scare some hipster pastors who have been avoiding these prayers because they're Oh, so scary. Enjoy and, rock and roll.

A Psalm of War Against Evil Leaders

A lot of people -- for many, many serious reasons -- are wringing their hands nowadays over the glide path our nation is tooling down thanks to the Marxist morons inside the Beltway.

Yep, at this writing, our current bevy of "elected" leaders care for that which is holy, just, and good about as much as badger cares what a prairie dog feels when he's chewing on its carotid artery.

I've personally seen and heard many Christians buy into this handwringing over the state of our union and I have wondered aloud, "Why don't you, dear Christian, cease to sweat these godless leaders and pray that God either convert them or take them out?"

Here in Psalm 2, David's not sweating a culture's smack-talking against God. He's not curled up in the fetal position, sucking his thumb, and wetting his pants over their godless and goofy plots to be free of God and cut loose from His law.

Matter of fact, David's reaction is just the opposite of what most doom-n-gloom Christians are boo-hooing about during these days of declension.

Indeed, David states that when rebel-kings start crap-talking God and attempt to dispense with His decrees -- that God mocks them. Yep, Jehovah's amused at these presumptive idiots who wish to lead a nation without giving God honor by adhering to His way.

And He doesn't just laugh, as you're about to see, He gets ticked off and that's bad news bears for the fools attempting to cast loose from God's gracious moorings.

Ergo, dear Christian, instead of chewing your fingernails down to the nub and buying the fear that saddles the faithless, why don't you pray out loud Psalm 2 that David prayed and penned many moons ago?

Psalm 2 (KJV)

Dear Christian: Your Fear is Full of Crap

1 Why do the heathen rage, and the people imagine a vain thing?

2 The kings of the earth set themselves, and the rulers take counsel together, against the Lord, and against his anointed, saying,

3 Let us break their bands asunder, and cast away their cords from us.

4 He that sitteth in the heavens shall laugh: the Lord shall have them in derision.

5 Then shall he speak unto them in his wrath, and vex them in his sore displeasure.

6 Yet have I set my king upon my holy hill of Zion.

7 I will declare the decree: the Lord hath said unto me, Thou art my Son; this day have I begot- ten thee.

8 Ask of me, and I shall give thee the heathen for thine inheritance, and the uttermost parts of the earth for thy possession.

9 Thou shalt break them with a rod of iron; thou shalt dash them in pieces like a potter's vessel.

6 Yet have I set my king upon my holy hill of Zion.

7 I will declare the decree: the Lord hath said unto me, Thou art my Son; this day have I begot- ten thee.

8 Ask of me, and I shall give thee the heathen for thine inheritance, and the uttermost parts of the earth for thy possession.

9 Thou shalt break them with a rod of iron; thou shalt dash them in pieces like a potter's vessel.

A Psalm of War Against Evil Schemers

Have you ever looked at clearly wicked, impenitent, people and leaders and think, "Why the heck are they prospering and their wretched schemes succeeding?"

In the meantime, in-between time, folks that are trying

to do right, obey God, and influence society with the gracious biblical worldview, are getting kicked by culture like a stuck door at Chuck Norris's house.

Yep, in today's jacked-up world, evil gets the green light and Christianity gets cancelled. It seems whacked and highly "unfair" that the aforementioned appears to be the case.

One would almost think that there is no God, or if there is one, He sure doesn't give one flibbertigibbet about what's going down on this third rock from the sun because the spawns of Satan seem to be winning and God's people are getting the shiitake mushrooms stomped out of them.

One thing for the Christian to consider before they get all gloomy and begin to make Van Gogh look like a rodeo clown is this: just because God isn't visibly kicking the wicked's backside, doesn't mean an ass-whuppin' is not coming.

David dealt with this dilemma in Psalm 10. The wicked during his day plotted against him and Israel. They taunted Jehovah. They defied the people of God. They hunted down the righteous. They scorned God and, seemingly, they were getting away with it. Yep, they were cocksure they would never be held accountable for their hellish actions. But that's where the malicious were wrong. As in, dead wrong.

Look at what David prayed at these hounds from hell. Pay particular attention to verses fifteen and sixteen.

Remember to pray Psalm 10 the next time you begin to think the wicked will get away with their wickedness and the righteous are doomed to be Satan's doormat.

Psalm 10 (KJV)

1 Why standest thou afar off, O Lord? why hidest thou thyself in times of trouble?

Dear Christian: Your Fear is Full of Crap

2 The wicked in his pride doth persecute the poor: let them be taken in the devices that they have imagined.

3 For the wicked boasteth of his heart's desire, and blesseth the covetous, whom the Lord abhor- reth.

4 The wicked, through the pride of his countenance, will not seek after God: God is not in all his thoughts.

5 His ways are always grievous; thy judgments are far above out of his sight: as for all his enemies, he puffeth at them.

6 He hath said in his heart, I shall not be moved: for I shall never be in adversity.

7 His mouth is full of cursing and deceit and fraud: under his tongue is mischief and vanity.

8 He sitteth in the lurking places of the villages: in the secret places doth he murder the innocent: his eyes are privily set against the poor.

9 He lieth in wait secretly as a lion in his den: he lieth in wait to catch the poor: he doth catch the poor, when he draweth him into his net.

10 He croucheth, and humbleth himself, that the poor may fall by his strong ones.

11 He hath said in his heart, God hath forgotten: he hideth his face; he will never see it.

12 Arise, O Lord; O God, lift up thine hand: for- get not the humble.

13 Wherefore doth the wicked contemn God? he hath said in his heart, Thou wilt not require it.

14 Thou hast seen it; for thou beholdest mischief and spite, to requite it with thy hand: the poor committeth himself unto thee; thou art the help- er of the fatherless.

15 Break thou the arm of the wicked and the evil man: seek out his wickedness till thou find none.

16 The Lord is King for ever and ever: the heathen are perished out of his land.

17 Lord, thou hast heard the desire of the humble: thou wilt prepare their heart, thou wilt cause thine ear to hear:

18 To judge the fatherless and the oppressed, that the man of the earth may no more oppress.

A Psalm of War Against the Slanderous

In our prissy current culture of wokeness, everyone is scared to death of getting on the wrong side of the pissants who make up the self-appointed Thought Police.

There're massive companies raking in millions helping people clean up old tweets, remove bad reviews about their person, or their goods, services, or merchandise.

People are terrified about being lied about or … gasp … possibly unliked on Google or social media.

David dealt with similar twaddle when he toured this blue marble. David, however, didn't have ReputationDefender.com to go to bat for him and clear up any hogwash his haters were spewing about him.

Yep, the giant killer didn't have a killer giant company to set the record straight and defend David's life before the fickle plebes who made up ancient Israel.

Poor David. What's a shepherd boy to do?

Well, what David lacked in the natural realm to contend against untoward foes, he made up for in spades in the supernatural realm having The Defender running interference for him.

Indeed, David called upon God, not Mark Zuckerberg, to sort out those who sought to sully his name.

If you're currently being lied about, or dasypygals are haranguing you by bringing up some past blunder, my advice would be to pull a Psalm 17 prayer out and shoot it heavenward and ask God to fight for you while you chill

Dear Christian: Your Fear is Full of Crap

and take a big nap at rest in His love.

Psalm 17 (KJV)

1 Hear a just cause, O Lord, give heed to my cry;

Give ear to my prayer, which is not from deceitful lips.

2 Let my judgment come forth from Your presence;

Let Your eyes look with equity.

3 You have tried my heart;

You have visited me by night;

You have tested me and You find nothing;

I have purposed that my mouth will not transgress.

4 As for the deeds of men, by the word of Your lips

I have kept from the paths of the violent.

5 My steps have held fast to Your paths. My feet have not slipped.

6 I have called upon You, for You will answer me, O God; Incline Your ear to me, hear my speech.

7 Wondrously show Your lovingkindness,

O Savior of those who take refuge at Your right hand From those who rise up against them.

8 Keep me as the apple of the eye; Hide me in the shadow of Your wings

9 From the wicked who despoil me, My deadly enemies who surround me.

10 They have closed their unfeeling heart, With their mouth they speak proudly.

11 They have now surrounded us in our steps; They set their eyes to cast us down to the ground.

12 He is like a lion that is eager to tear, And as a young lion lurking in hiding places.

13 Arise, O Lord, confront him, bring him low; Deliver my soul from the wicked with Your sword,

14 From men with Your hand, O Lord,

From men of the world, whose portion is in this life,

And whose belly You fill with Your treasure; They are satisfied with children,

And leave their abundance to their babes.

15 As for me, I shall behold Your face in righteousness;

I will be satisfied with Your likeness when I awake.

A Psalm of War Against those Who Hate the Righteous

If you're worth your salt, then you're going to be attacked more viciously than a case of Twinkies would be at a Rosie O'Donnell plus-sized slumber party.

I know they didn't tell you that at Leitaphart Community Church, but it is true. Jesus said, "If they hated me, they're going to hate you." And you would've known that if you had read your Bible. Anyway ...

David was no stranger to hatred.

If the shepherd boy was around today slinging stones, beheading giants, and singing epic songs that literally exorcise devils from peoples' persons, he would be as ardently loved and vehemently loathed as he was 3,000 years ago.

Dealing with such a dichotomy of love and wrath can scramble your eggs.

It can make it difficult to know who to turn to for soul support.

Who the heck can you trust?

The "people of God", throughout David's life, were a main source of persecution. In other words, David ain't gonna get any solace unbearing his heavy burdens at the men's group meeting because most of those bastards hated him, were untrustworthy, and were longing for his demise.

Sometimes, oft times, and I know this isn't what Oprah would say, you the Christian, have to go at it alone with God. Some people think the aforementioned is so sad. I think it's so cool. Isn't that what Christianity is all about, knowing God and trusting Him and Him alone?

David trusted God and lifted up his soul to Him, at the exclusion of others, and asked the Lord, and Him alone, to not let his enemies get the upper hand and to not let him be ashamed.

Meditate on those first two verses in Psalm 25 and then enjoy the rest of this substantial song.

Psalm 25 (KJV)

1 Unto thee, O Lord, do I lift up my soul.

2 O my God, I trust in thee: let me not be ashamed, let not mine enemies triumph over me.

3 Yea, let none that wait on thee be ashamed: let them be ashamed which transgress without cause.

4 Shew me thy ways, O Lord; teach me thy paths.

5 Lead me in thy truth, and teach me: for thou art the God of my salvation; on thee do I wait all the day.

6 Remember, O Lord, thy tender mercies and thy loving-kindnesses; for they have been ever of old.

7 Remember not the sins of my youth, nor my transgressions: according to thy mercy remember thou me for thy goodness' sake, O Lord.

8 Good and upright is the Lord: therefore will he teach sinners in the way.

9 The meek will he guide in judgment: and the meek will he teach his way.

10 All the paths of the Lord are mercy and truth unto such as keep his covenant and his testimonies.

11 For thy name's sake, O Lord, pardon mine iniquity; for it is great.

12 What man is he that feareth the Lord? him shall he teach in the way that he shall choose.

13 His soul shall dwell at ease; and his seed shall inherit the earth.

14 The secret of the Lord is with them that fear him; and he will shew them his covenant.

15 Mine eyes are ever toward the Lord; for he shall pluck my feet out of the net.

16 Turn thee unto me, and have mercy upon me; for I am desolate and afflicted.

17 The troubles of my heart are enlarged: O bring thou me out of my distresses.

A Psalm of War Against Anti-Christian Blowhards

China hates America.

Iran's no fan either.

Ditto with Russia.

And mega-dittos regarding George Soros.

Yes, America and her Constitution, Bill of Rights, and our Declaration of Independence are a thing of fear and loathing for our enemies foreign and domestic.

The true Church also draws deep disdain from the aforementioned and you can add to that list Marxist radicals who've embraced an anti-theistic worldview of stupidity on steroids.

Indeed, these ideological bedfellows don't like those who call upon the Lord with an unfeigned faith and from a pure heart.

Dear Christian: Your Fear is Full of Crap

Ergo, they plot to do the Church in. They conspire how to crush us. They'd like to see us wiped off the face of this earth with the Church's name scratched off the books.

That's where Psalm 83 comes in real handy.

Asaph, in Psalm 83, prays to God to do this to their new set of enemies what God did to the old set of enemies such as, Edom, Moab, Gebal, Ammon, Amalek, Philistia, The Tyrians, Assyria, and the Midianites.

Google what God did to His people's enemies who wouldn't leave His Chosen Ones alone. It wasn't pretty.

Ps. 83:13-18 is what the Church should pray against the powers of darkness and their earthly ilk who persecute the church and will not repent.

Psalm 83 (KJV)

1 Keep not thou silence, O God: hold not thy peace, and be not still, O God.

2 For, lo, thine enemies make a tumult: and they that hate thee have lifted up the head.

3 They have taken crafty counsel against thy peo- ple, and consulted against thy hidden ones.

4 They have said, Come, and let us cut them off from being a nation; that the name of Israel may be no more in remembrance.

5 For they have consulted together with one con- sent: they are confederate against thee:

6 The tabernacles of Edom, and the Ishmaelites; of Moab, and the Hagarenes;

7 Gebal, and Ammon, and Amalek; the Philis- tines with the inhabitants of Tyre;

8 Assur also is joined with them: they have hol- pen the children of Lot. Selah.

9 Do unto them as unto the Midianites; as to Si- sera, as to Jabin, at the brook of Kison:

10 Which perished at Endor: they became as dung for the earth.

11 Make their nobles like Oreb, and like Zeeb: yea, all their princes as Zebah, and as Zalmunna:

12 Who said, Let us take to ourselves the houses of God in possession.

13 O my God, make them like a wheel; as the stubble before the wind.

14 As the fire burneth a wood, and as the flame setteth the mountains on fire;

15 So persecute them with thy tempest, and make them afraid with thy storm.

16 Fill their faces with shame; that they may seek thy name, O Lord.

17 Let them be confounded and troubled for ever; yea, let them be put to shame, and perish:

18 That men may know that thou, whose name alone is Jehovah, art the most high over all the earth.

Culture Warrior Battle Notes

Chapter Twenty: Satan Doesn't Want You Reading This Chapter

"My main ambition in life is to be on the Devil's most wanted list."
– Leonard Ravenhill

The thief comes only to steal and kill and destroy; I came so that they would have life, and [a]have it abundantly. John 10:10 (NASB)

According to Christ, the thief (ie., Satan, his defeated ilk, bad politicians, big tech control freaks, Fake News talking heads and the self-righteous religious dorks he possesses) come to steal, kill, and destroy and we saw a lot of their devastation from 2020-2021+.

Lots of destruction of businesses, churches, personal income, hopes, and dreams ruined. Crushed in a scant few months.

Currently, in 2022, we're seeing our great nation getting gutted like a fish by enemies of our Constitution, Bill of Rights, and our Declaration of Independence.

This massive theft and destruction of our cherished liberties has left folks ticked off and depressed.

Where Satan wreaks havoc, God counters (Rom. 5:20) with His restorative power and when God restores our lives, His Church, and our Nation it is always better in quality, quantity, and kind.

For all of you who've been ripped off and devastated by the enemy, check this scripture/biblical principle out …

> *30 Excuses might be found for a thief who steals because he is starving.*
>
> *31 But if he is caught, he must pay back seven times what he stole, even if he has to sell everything in his house. Prov. 6:30-31 (NLT)*

What does Solomon say a thief has to do if he's caught thieving?

He says the thief has to restore seven times the amount he ripped off.

Restoration is a mondo-theme throughout the Bible. It's bigger than Dallas. It's impossible to miss. When God's people got trounced by the enemy and even by their own stupid mistakes, God swoops in, smashes the forces of darkness, and restores unto His covenant kids what they have had taken from them by *el Diablo*.

Throughout the scripture we see the hand of God restore His people's health, wealth, position, land, His Church and our souls.

Plow through this epic list of God's promises and declare them with holy boldness over your life, our Nation and His Church and watch God start moving in restorative power over all the hurt hell has brought to your doorstep.

Dear Christian: Your Fear is Full of Crap

God Restores Our Health. If your health has taken a hit via the poison that was unleashed upon the world from Wuhan, ask God to restore your health like He did to the following folks.

Then He said, "Put your hand inside the fold of your robe again." So he put his hand into the fold again, and when he took it out of the fold, behold, it was restored like the rest of his flesh. Exod. 4:7 (NASB)

May he also be to you one who restores life and sustains your old age; for your daughter-in-law, who loves you and is better to you than seven sons, has given birth to him. Ruth 4:15) (NASB)

And the king responded and said to the man of God, "Please appease the Lord your God and pray for me, so that my hand may be restored to me." So the man of God appeased the Lord, and the king's hand was restored to him, and it became as it was before. 1Kings 13:6 (NASB)

And Elisha sent a messenger to him, saying, "Go and wash in the Jordan seven times, and your flesh will be restored to you and you will be clean. 2Kngs 5:10 (NASB)

So he went down and dipped himself in the Jordan seven times, in accordance with the word of the man of God; and his flesh was restored like the flesh of a little child, and he was clean. 2Kings 5:14 (NASB)

And as he was reporting to the king how he had restored to life the one who was dead, behold, the woman whose son he had restored to life appealed to the king for her house and for her field. And Gehazi said, "My lord the king, this is the woman and this is her son, whom Elisha restored to life. 2Kings 8:5 (NASB)

The Lord will sustain him upon his sickbed; In his illness, You restore him to health. Ps. 41:3 (NASB)

Lord, by these things people live, And in all these is the life of my spirit; Restore me to health and let me live. Isa. 38:16 (NASB)

For I will restore you to health And I will heal you of your wounds,' declares the Lord, 'Because they have called you an outcast, saying: "It is Zion; no one cares for her. Jer. 30:17 (NASB)

Then He said to the man, "Stretch out your hand!" He stretched it out, and it was restored to normal, like the other. Matt. 12:13 (NASB)

So the crowd was astonished as they saw those who were unable to speak talking, those with impaired limbs restored, those who were limping walking around, and those who were blind seeing; and they glorified the God of Israel. Matt. 15:31 (NASB)

Then again He laid His hands on his eyes; and he looked intently and was restored, and began to see everything clearly. Mark 8:25 (NASB)

And the prayer of faith will restore the one who is sick, and the Lord will raise him up, and if he has committed sins, they will be forgiven him. James 5:15 (NASB)

God Restores Our Wealth. If you got wiped financially during the Bad Cold Charade ask God to restore your finances like He did here …

When the king asked the woman, she told everything to him. So the king appointed an officer for her, saying, "Restore all that was hers and all the produce of the field from the day that she left the land even until now. 2Kings 8:6 (NASB)

Dear Christian: Your Fear is Full of Crap

The Lord also restored the fortunes of Job when he prayed for his friends, and the Lord increased double all that Job had. Job 42:10 (NASB)

Oh, that the salvation of Israel would come out of Zion! When the Lord restores the fortunes of His people, Jacob will rejoice, Israel will be glad. Ps. 14:7 (NASB)

Oh, that the salvation of Israel would come from Zion! When God restores the fortunes of His people, Jacob shall rejoice, Israel shall be glad. Ps. 53:6 (NASB)

Lord, You showed favor to Your land; You restored the fortunes of Jacob. Ps. 85:1 (NASB)

Restore our fortunes, Lord, As the streams in the South. Ps. 126:4 (NASB)

For behold, days are coming,' declares the Lord, 'when I will restore the fortunes of My people Israel and Judah.' The Lord says, 'I will also bring them back to the land that I gave to their forefathers, and they shall take possession of it. Jer. 30:3 (NASB)

"This is what the Lord says: 'Behold, I will restore the fortunes of the tents of Jacob And have compassion on his dwellings; And the city will be rebuilt on its ruins, And the palace will stand on its rightful place. Jer. 30:18 (NASB)

This is what the Lord of armies, the God of Israel says: "Once again they will speak this word in the land of Judah and in its cities when I restore their fortunes, 'The Lord bless you, O place of righteousness, O holy hill! Jer. 31:23 (NASB)

People will buy fields for money, sign and seal deeds, and call in witnesses in the land of Benjamin, in the areas surrounding Jerusalem, in the cities of

Judah, in the cities of the hill country, in the cities of the lowland, and in the cities of the Negev; for I will restore their fortunes,' declares the Lord." Jer. 32:44 (NASB)

And I will restore the fortunes of Judah and the fortunes of Israel, and will rebuild them as they were at first. Jer. 33:7 (NASB)

The voice of joy and the voice of gladness, the voice of the groom and the voice of the bride, the voice of those who say, "Give thanks to the Lord of armies, For the Lord is good, For His mercy is everlasting," as they bring a thanksgiving offering into the house of the Lord. For I will restore the fortunes of the land as they were at first,' says the Lord. Jer. 33:11 (NASB)

Then I would reject the descendants of Jacob and David My servant, so as not to take from his descendants rulers over the descendants of Abraham, Isaac, and Jacob. But I will restore their fortunes and have mercy on them. Jer. 33:26 (NASB)

Yet I will restore the fortunes of Moab In the latter days," declares the Lord. This is the extent of the judgment on Moab Jer. 48:47 (NASB)

But afterward I will restore The fortunes of the sons of Ammon," Declares the Lord. Jer. 49:6 (NASB)

'But it will come about in the last days That I will restore the fortunes of Elam,'" Declares the Lord. Jer. 49:39 (NASB)

Therefore this is what the Lord God says: "Now I will restore the fortunes of Jacob and have mercy on all the house of Israel; and I will be jealous for My holy name. Ezek. 39:25 (NASB)

Dear Christian: Your Fear is Full of Crap

*Also, Judah, there is a harvest appointed for you,
When I restore the fortunes of My people. Hosea
6:11 (NASB)*

*I will also restore the fortunes of My people Israel,
And they will rebuild the desolated cities and live in
them; They will also plant vineyards and drink their
wine, And make gardens and eat their fruit. Amos
9:14 (NASB)*

God Restores Our Position. If you lost a job because
your conscience disallowed you to obey the edicts of goof-
balls with way too much power, ask Jehovah to restore your
position in life or give you a better gig as He did here ...

*Within three more days Pharaoh will lift up your
head and restore you to your office; and you will
put Pharaoh's cup into his hand as in your former
practice when you were his cupbearer Gen. 40:13
(NASB)*

*He restored the chief cupbearer to his office, and he
put the cup into Pharaoh's hand Gen. 40:21 (NASB)*

*And just as he interpreted for us, so it happened;
Pharaoh restored me in my office, but he hanged the
chief baker. Gen. 41:13 (NASB)*

*then the Lord your God will restore you from cap-
tivity, and have compassion on you, and will gather
you again from all the peoples where the Lord your
God has scattered you. Deut. 30:3 (NASB)*

*Then David said to him, "Do not be afraid, for I
will assuredly show kindness to you for the sake of
your father Jonathan, and I will restore to you all
the land of your grandfather Saul; and you yourself
shall eat at my table regularly. 2Sam. 9:7 (NASB)*

If you are pure and upright, Surely now He will stir Himself for you and restore your righteous estate. Job 8:6 (NASB)

If you return to the Almighty, you will be restored; If you remove injustice far from your tent. Job 22:23 (NASB)

Then he will pray to God, and He will accept him, So that he may see His face with joy, And He will restore His righteousness to that person. Job 33:26 (NASB)

Therefore, this is what the Lord says: "If you return, then I will restore you— You will stand before Me; And if you extract the precious from the worthless, You will become My spokesman. They, for their part, may turn to you, But as for you, you are not to turn to them. Jer. 15:19 (NASB)

I will also show you compassion, so that he will have compassion on you and restore you to your own soil. Jer. 42:12 (NASB)

At that time my reason returned to me. And my majesty and splendor were restored to me for the honor of my kingdom, and my state counselors and my nobles began seeking me out; so I was reestablished in my sovereignty, and surpassing greatness was added to me. Dan. 4:36 (NASB)

For the Lord will restore the splendor of Jacob Like the splendor of Israel, Even though destroyers have laid waste to them And ruined their vines. Nah. 2:2 (NASB)

God Restores Our Land. Instead of thinking that our land is irreparably screwed, believe God to heal our great Nation like He's done before. Pray and declare these awesome verses.

Dear Christian: Your Fear is Full of Crap

The cities which the Philistines had taken from Israel were restored to Israel, from Ekron even to Gath; and Israel recovered their territory from the hand of the Philistines. So there was peace between Israel and the Amorites. 1Sam. 7:14 (NASB)

He says, "It is too small a thing that You should be My Servant To raise up the tribes of Jacob and to restore the protected ones of Israel; I will also make You a light of the nations So that My salvation may reach to the end of the earth." Isa. 49:6 (NASB)

This is what the Lord says: "At a favorable time I answered You, And on a day of salvation I helped You; And I will watch over You and make You a covenant of the people, To restore the land, to give as inheritances the deserted hereditary lands. Isa. 49:8 (NASB)

but, 'As the Lord lives, who brought up the sons of Israel from the land of the north and from all the lands where He had banished them.' For I will restore them to their own land which I gave to their fathers. Jer. 16:15 (NASB)

"They will be brought to Babylon and will be there until the day I visit them," declares the Lord. "Then I will bring them back and restore them to this place. Jer. 27:22 (NASB)

God Restores The House of God. A whole stack of churches are woke and beholden to big government tools. Pray that God will restore His Church like He did the House of the Lord back in the OT.

Now it came about after this that Joash decided to restore the house of the Lord. 2Chron. 24:4 (NASB)

The king and Jehoiada gave it to those who did the work of the service of the house of the Lord; and they hired masons and carpenters to restore the house of the Lord, and also workers in iron and bronze to repair the house of the Lord. 2Chron. 24:12 (NASB)

For we are slaves; yet in our bondage our God has not abandoned us, but has extended favor to us in the sight of the kings of Persia, to give us reviving to erect the house of our God, to restore its ruins, and to give us a wall in Judah and Jerusalem. Ezek. 9:9 (NASB)

God, restore us And make Your face shine upon us, and we will be saved. Ps. 80:3 (NASB)

Restore us, God of our salvation, And cause Your indignation toward us to cease. Ps. 85:4 (NASB)

Listen! Your watchmen raise their voices, They shout joyfully together; For they will see with their own eyes When the Lord restores Zion. Isa. 52:8 (NASB)

Those from among you will rebuild the ancient ruins; You will raise up the age-old foundations; And you will be called the repairer of the breach, The restorer of the streets in which to dwell. Isa. 58:12 (NASB)

Then I will restore your judges as at first, And your counselors as at the beginning; After that you will be called the city of righteousness, A faithful city. Isa. 1:26 (NASB)

I will let Myself be found by you,' declares the Lord, 'and I will restore your fortunes and gather you from all the nations and all the places where I have driven you,' declares the Lord, 'and I will bring you back to the place from where I sent you into exile Jer. 29:14 (NASB)

Restore us to You, Lord, so that we may be restored; Renew our days as of old. Lam. 5:21 (NASB)

For then I will restore to the peoples pure lips, So that all of them may call on the name of the Lord, To serve Him shoulder to shoulder Zeph. 3:9 (NASB)

At that time I will bring you in, Even at the time when I gather you together; Indeed, I will make you famous and praiseworthy Among all the peoples of the earth, When I restore your fortunes before your eyes," Says the Lord. Zeph. 3:20 (NASB)

'After these things I will return, And I will rebuild the fallen tabernacle of David, And I will rebuild its ruins, And I will restore it. Acts 15:16 (NASB)

God Restores Our Soul. If you got your soul sucked dry in the last couple of years because of all the mass delusional psychosis that was pumped into our noggins, 24/7/365, shout these promises from your rooftop.

He restores my soul; He guides me in the paths of righteousness For the sake of His name. Ps. 23:3 (NASB)

Restore to me the joy of Your salvation, And sustain me with a willing spirit. Ps. 51:12 (NASB)

God, You have rejected us. You have broken us; You have been angry; restore us! Ps. 60:1 (NASB)

I have seen his ways, but I will heal him; I will lead him and restore comfort to him and to his mourners Isa. 57:18 (NASB)

I have certainly heard Ephraim grieving, 'You have disciplined me, and I was corrected, Like an untrained calf; Bring me back that I may be restored, For You are the Lord my God. Jer. 31:18 (NASB)

Then I will compensate you for the years That the swarming locust has eaten, The creeping locust, the stripping locust, and the gnawing locust— My great army which I sent among you. Joel 2:25 (NASB)

Return to the stronghold, you prisoners who have the hope; This very day I am declaring that I will restore double to you. Zech. 9:12 (NASB)

Brothers and sisters, even if a person is caught in any wrongdoing, you who are spiritual are to restore such a person in a spirit of gentleness; each one looking to yourself, so that you are not tempted as well. Gal. 6:1 (NASB)

Finally, here's some more yummy nuggets to declare over your life, home, God's Church and our Nation. Renew your mind with these magnificent promises instead of the bullcrap Fake News spewers launch at us every second of the day.

"For I will restore health to you, and your wounds I will heal," declares the Lord, "because they have called you an outcast: 'It is Zion, for whom no one cares!'" Jer. 30:17 (NASB)

Restore to me the joy of your salvation, and uphold me with a willing spirit. Ps. 51:12 (NASB)

Instead of your shame there shall be a double portion; instead of dishonor they shall rejoice in their lot; therefore in their land they shall possess a double portion; they shall have everlasting joy. Isa. 61:7 (NASB)

Dear Christian: Your Fear is Full of Crap

And after you have suffered a little while, the God of all grace, who has called you to his eternal glory in Christ, will himself restore, confirm, strengthen, and establish you. 1Pet. 5:10 (NASB)

For everyone who has been born of God overcomes the world. And this is the victory that has overcome the world—our faith. 1John 5:4 (NASB)

If my people who are called by my name humble themselves, and pray and seek my face and turn from their wicked ways, then I will hear from heaven and will forgive their sin and heal their land. 2Chron. 7:14 (NASB)

And when the king asked the woman, she told him. So the king appointed an official for her, saying, "Restore all that was hers, together with all the produce of the fields from the day that she left the land until now." 2Kings 8:6 (NASB)

I will seek the lost, and I will bring back the strayed, and I will bind up the injured, and I will strengthen the weak, and the fat and the strong I will destroy. I will feed them in justice. Ezek. 34:16 (NASB)

"Come, let us return to the Lord; for he has torn us, that he may heal us; he has struck us down, and he will bind us up." Hosea 6:1 (ESV)

But they who wait for the Lord shall renew their strength; they shall mount up with wings like eagles; they shall run and not be weary; they shall walk and not faint. Isa. 40:31 (ESV)

Therefore, confess your sins to one another and pray for one another, that you may be healed. The prayer of a righteous person has great power as it is working. James 5:16 (ESV)

Heal me, O Lord, and I shall be healed; save me, and I shall be saved, for you are my praise. Jer. 17:14 (ESV)

I will give them a heart to know that I am the Lord, and they shall be my people and I will be their God, for they shall return to me with their whole heart. Jer. 24:7 (ESV)

For I know the plans I have for you, declares the Lord, plans for welfare and not for evil, to give you a future and a hope. Jer. 29:11 (ESV)

"Behold, I am the Lord, the God of all flesh. Is anything too hard for me?" Jer. 32:27 (ESV)

"Have I not commanded you? Be strong and courageous. Do not be frightened, and do not be dismayed, for the Lord your God is with you wherever you go." Josh. 1:9 (ESV)

"The Spirit of the Lord is upon me, because he has anointed me to proclaim good news to the poor. He has sent me to proclaim liberty to the captives and recovering of sight to the blind, to set at liberty those who are oppressed." Luke 4:18 (ESV)

"Therefore I tell you, whatever you ask in prayer, believe that you have received it, and it will be yours." Mark 11:24 (ESV)

Then Jesus laid his hands on his eyes again; and he opened his eyes, his sight was restored, and he saw everything clearly. Mark 8:25 (ESV)

"Again I say to you, if two of you agree on earth about anything they ask, it will be done for them by my Father in heaven." Matt. 18:19 (ESV)

Dear Christian: Your Fear is Full of Crap

"But seek first the kingdom of God and his righteousness, and all these things will be added to you." Matt. 6:33 (ESV)

The Lord upholds all who are falling and raises up all who are bowed down. Ps. 145:14 (ESV)

Cast me not away from your presence, and take not your Holy Spirit from me. Ps. 51:1) (ESV)

Purge me with hyssop, and I shall be clean; wash me, and I shall be whiter than snow. Ps. 51:7 (ESV)

You let men ride over our heads; we went through fire and through water; yet you have brought us out to a place of abundance. Ps. 66:12 (ESV)

You who have made me see many troubles and calamities will revive me again; from the depths of the earth you will bring me up again. Ps. 71:20 (ESV)

May the God of hope fill you with all joy and peace in believing, so that by the power of the Holy Spirit you may abound in hope. Rom. 15:13 (ESV)

And we know that for those who love God all things work together for good, for those who are called according to his purpose. Rom. 8:28 (ESV)

One more thing. If some killjoy, religious naysayer says, "These promises aren't for you but for other people at other times" remind them of these scriptures.

All scripture is given by inspiration of God, and is profitable for doctrine, for reproof, for correction, for instruction in righteousness: That the man of God may be perfect, thoroughly furnished unto all good works. 2Tim. 3:16,17 (KJV)

For whatsoever things were written aforetime were written for our learning, that we through patience and comfort of the scriptures might have hope. Rom. 15:4 (KJV)

2 Corinthians 1:20 For all the promises of God in him are yea, and in him Amen, unto the glory of God by us. 2Cor. 1:20 (KJV)

2 Grace and peace be multiplied unto you through the knowledge of God, and of Jesus our Lord, 3 According as his divine power hath given unto us all things that pertain unto life and godliness, through the knowledge of him that hath called us to glory and virtue: 4 Whereby are given unto us exceeding great and precious promises: that by these ye might be partakers of the divine nature, having escaped the corruption that is in the world through lust. 2Pet. 1:2-4 (KJV)

In addition, tell the cold-water bucket brigade to google Malachi 3:6, James 1:17, and Hebrews 13:8 if they think God's changed and He's not in the miraculous restoration business anymore.

Culture Warrior Battle Notes

Doug Giles

The Biblical Badass Collection

Here's my ever-growing collection of Biblical Badasses that I've depicted with this stuff called "oil paint". I loathe how artists have made the men and women of the scripture look like demure punching bags for the powers of darkness when they were everything but that. Some of the originals are still available. We have prints of all of them ranging from small to T-Rex-sized wall monsters. We print on luster paper, museum quality canvas, wood, and for all you metal-heads, we print on metal as well. To check out all of my paintings, aside from this collection, log on to DougGiles. Art. Enjoy.

Esther

Christ Clearing the Temple

Zipporah

Christ Confronts the Pharisees

Rahab the Harlot

Jael

Samson before Delilah

Samson after Delilah

More than a Prophet

Solomon

Moses

Prodigal Son

John the Baptist: The Kingdom Suffers Violence

COMETH

Judgment Cometh

Full Armor #

Full Armor #2

The 12

Jacob Wrestling an Angel

Jesus Just before He Cleansed the Temple

Elijah the Wildman

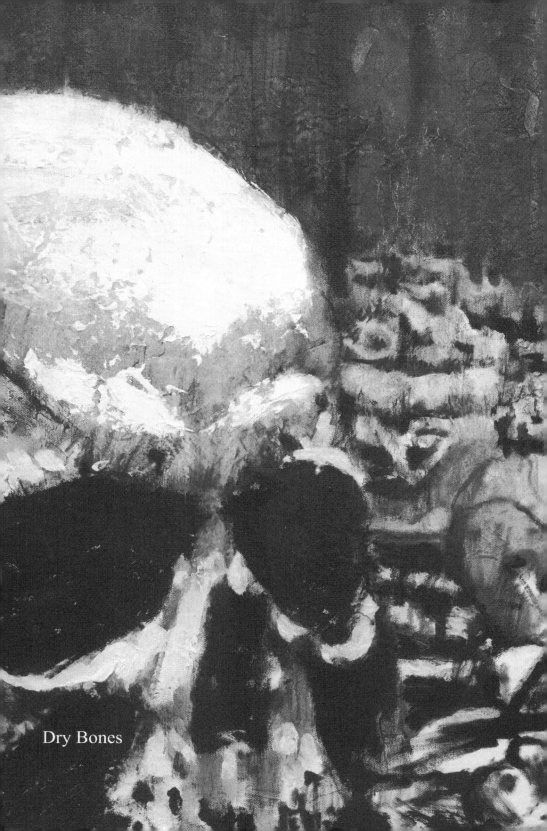

Dry Bones

David: 1 Samuel 17

Mary

giles
3/2

Deborah

About the Author

Doug earned his Bachelor of Fine Arts degree from Texas Tech University and his certificates in both Theological and Biblical Studies from Knox Theological Seminary (Dr. D. James Kennedy, Chancellor). Giles was fortunate to have Dr. R.C. Sproul as an instructor for many classes.

Doug Giles is the host of The Doug Giles Podcast, the co-founder and co-host of the Warriors & Wildmen podcast (1M downloads) and the man behind ClashDaily.com. In addition to driving Clash-Daily.com (270M+ page views), Giles is the author of several #1 Amazon bestsellers including his most recent book, Psalms of War: Prayers That Literally Kick Ass. In 2018, Giles was permanently banned from his two-million followers on Facebook.

Doug is also an artist and a filmmaker and his online gallery can be seen at DougGiles.Art. His first film, Biblical Badasses: A Raw Look at Christianity and Art, is available via DougGiles.Art.

Doug's writings have appeared in several other print and online news sources, including Townhall.com, The Washington Times, The Daily Caller, Fox Nation, Human Events, USA Today, The Wall Street Journal, The Washington Examiner, American Hunter Magazine, and ABC News.

Giles and his wife Margaret have two daughters, Hannah and Regis. Hannah devastated ACORN with her 2009 nation-shaking undercover videos and she currently stars in the explosive 2018 Tribeca Documentary, Acorn and The Firestorm.

Regis has been featured in Elle, American Hunter, and Variety magazines. Regis is also the author of a powerful new book titled, How Not To Be A #Me-Too Victim, But A #WarriorChick.

Regis and Hannah are both black belts in Gracie/Valente Jiu-Jitsu.

Doug Giles

Speaking Engagements

Doug Giles speaks to college, business, community, church, advocacy, and men's groups throughout the United States and internationally. His expertise includes issues of Christianity and culture, masculinity vs. the wussification of the American male, God and government, big game hunting and fishing, raising righteous kids in a rank culture, the Second Amendment, personal empowerment, and social change. To invite Doug to speak at your next event, log on to DougGiles.org and fill out the invitation request.

Dear Christian: Your Fear is Full of Crap

Accolades for Giles include …

– Giles was recognized as one of "The 50 Best Conservative Columnists Of 2015"

– Giles was recognized as one of "The 50 Best Conservative Columnists Of 2014"

– Giles was recognized as one of "The 50 Best Conservative Columnists Of 2013"

– ClashDaily.com was recognized as one of "The 100 Most Popular Conservative Websites For 2013 and 2020"

– Doug was noted as "Hot Conservative New Media Superman" By Politichicks

Between 2002 – 2006, Doug's 3-minute daily commentary in Miami received seven Silver Microphone Awards and two Communicator Awards.

Doug's podcast can be seen and heard at
ClashRadio.com.

Books by Doug Giles

Psalms of War: Prayers That Literally Kick Ass

Biblical Badasses: The Women

If Masculinity is 'Toxic,' Call Jesus Radioactive

Would Jesus Vote For Trump?

Rules For Radical Christians: 10 Biblical Disciplines for Influential Believers

Pussification: The Effeminization Of The American Male

Raising Righteous And Rowdy Girls

Raising Boys Feminists Will Hate

Rise, Kill and Eat: A Theology of Hunting From Genesis to Revelation.

If You're Going Through Hell, Keep Going

My Grandpa is a Patriotic Badass

A Coloring Book for College Cry Babies

Sandy Hook Massacre: When Seconds Count, Police Are Minutes Away

The Bulldog Attitude: Get It or ... Get Left Behind

A Time To Clash

10 Habits of Decidedly Defective People: The Successful Loser's Guide to Life

Political Twerps, Cultural Jerks, Church Quirks

Doug Giles

Theologians call these specific prayers, from the psalmist David, "imprecatory prayers." They are prayers to pull out and pray when things get bad -- as in real bad. Prayers you use when a nation's getting mucked up by degenerate priests or politicians, or when the enemy is crushing the people of God, or when your flesh/personal demons are out of control.

King David was the king of this type of incendiary intercession. This giant killer slayed more Goliaths in his prayers and songs than he ever did with a rock and slingshot. Oh, and by the way, Jesus said all those imprecations David dealt out were not the mad ramblings of a ticked off warrior poet, but were actually inspired by the Holy Spirit. (See Matthew 22:43.)

Psalms of War: Prayers That Literally Kick Ass is a compendium from the book of Psalms, regarding how David rolled in prayer. I bet you haven't heard these read, prayed or sang in church against our formidable enemies, have you? I didn't think so. It might be time to dust them off and offer 'em up if you're truly concerned about the state of Christ's Church and our nation.

Also included in this book, Psalms of War, are full-color reproductions of the author's original art from his Biblical Badass Series of oil paintings.

Made in the USA
Monee, IL
20 July 2022

10051683R00144